START HERE START HERE NOW

D0707831

# Liz Kleinrock

# START HERE START NOW

## A Guide to Antibias and Antiracist Work in Your School Community

**HEINEMANN**
Portsmouth, NH

**Heinemann**

145 Maplewood Avenue, Suite 300

Portsmouth, NH 03801

www.heinemann.com

*Offices and agents throughout the world*

© 2021 by Elizabeth Kleinrock

All rights reserved. No part of this book may be reproduced in any form or by any electronic or mechanical means, including information storage and retrieval systems, without permission in writing from the publisher, except by a reviewer, who may quote brief passages in a review, and with the exception of reproducible pages (identified by the *Start Here, Start Now* copyright line), which may be photocopied for classroom use only.

> *Heinemann's authors have devoted their entire careers to developing the unique content in their works, and their written expression is protected by copyright law. We respectfully ask that you do not adapt, reuse, or copy anything on third-party (whether for-profit or not-for-profit) lesson-sharing websites.*
> **—Heinemann Publishers**

"Dedicated to Teachers" is a trademark of Greenwood Publishing Group, Inc.

The author and publisher wish to thank those who have generously given permission to reprint borrowed material:

Figures 2–1 and 8–2: National Research Council. 2012. *A Framework for K–12 Science Education: Practices, Crosscutting Concepts, and Core Ideas*. Washington, DC: The National Academies Press. https://doi.org/10.17226/13165.

*Acknowledgments for borrowed material continue on p. 154.*

Library of Congress Control Number: 2021932791

ISBN-13: 978-0-325-11864-2

Editor: Holly Kim Price
Production: Vicki Kasabian
Cover design: Suzanne Heiser
Interior design and art creation: Shawn Girsberger
Author photo: Maya Fiellin
Photograph for Figure 7–7: Melissa Renwick/Toronto Star via Getty Images
Typesetter: Shawn Girsberger
Manufacturing: Val Cooper

Printed in the United States of American on acid-free paper
4  5  6  MP  26  25  24  23  22  21
October 2021 Printing

Dedicated to
Jamie Mackin, Corinne Wise Weitzman, and Stephanie Bloom,
for giving your hearts and souls
to our children and our community.

I miss you every day.

# CONTENTS

# ➡ ONLINE RESOURCES CONTENTS

**Online Resources for *Start Here, Start Now* can be found under Companion Resources at http://hein.pub/StartHereStartNow.**

# ➡ ACKNOWLEDGMENTS

Whatever we learn has a purpose and whatever we do affects everything and everyone else, if even in the tiniest way. Why, when a housefly flaps his wings, a breeze goes round the world; when a speck of dust falls to the ground, the entire planet weighs a little more; and when you stamp your foot, the earth moves slightly off its course. Whenever you laugh, gladness spreads like the ripples in the pond; and whenever you're sad, no one anywhere can be really happy. And it's much the same thing with knowledge, for whenever you learn something new, the whole world becomes that much richer.

—NORTON JUSTER'S *The Phantom Tollbooth*

## THIS BOOK IS HARDLY THE PRODUCT OF ONE PERSON'S LOVE AND LABOR.

This is a communal project and represents many of the voices who have shaped me as an educator and as a member of the community. Whether or not they are directly quoted in the pages, all of these people have pushed me to learn, unlearn, reflect, and grow through times of accomplishment and discomfort.

I have been so privileged to have learned from the works of educators, activists, and writers such as Yuri Kochiyama, Grace Lee Boggs, Carlos Bulosan, Gloria Anzaldúa, Audre Lorde, bell hooks, James Baldwin, adrienne maree brown, Bettina Love, Dr. Dena Simmons, Gholdy Muhammad, Louise Derman-Sparks, Julie Olsen Edwards, and countless others who have paved the way for myself and others by sharing your brilliance and stories.

To the Heinemann team, thank you for your support throughout this process! If I went back in time and told my student self that one day I'd write a book, I would have never believed it. Thank you for helping make my vision become a reality. A particularly huge shout-out to my editor Holly Kim Price, for taking notice of my work and giving me this chance to share it with the world. It has been such an honor to have your input and guidance on this journey.

To my colleagues and collaborators who talked to me about this book, Sara, Melissa, Tayo, Sandy, Katherine, Jessie, Jamilah, Denise, Adele, Natalie, Ace, Tooley, Angela, Chris, José, Cornelius, Amy, Bria, Charity, Emily, Charlie, Jessica, Cody, Kelly, Loretta, Anna, Makai, Natalie, Naomi, Jasmine, Dylan, Allie, Teresa, Sarah. When I think about all of the work you're doing in your schools and communities, the future feels a lot more secure. Thank you for sharing your time and expertise so others can learn.

To the CWCSL family. It was during my seven years as a founding teacher that I developed my authentic voice and style as a teacher. Thank you, Dr. Ramona, for taking a chance on me as a novice teacher, and to you and Dr. Maureen for creating a space where I could experiment and grow alongside my students. Thank you to Alison, without your influence, my classroom door might have stayed shut. I am so grateful to have worked and learned with you. Thank you for encouraging me to share my work when I didn't see or understand its value. To all of my co-teachers throughout my years at CWC, with a special shout-out to Meg, Emily, Shay, Lyndsay, Phil, Charlotte, Kirsten, Yun, and Jake. Thank you for being collaborators in this work and being patient with me.

To the Liberate & Chill crew. Working with and falling in love with all of you has been a turning point in my personal and professional life. The past year has been some of the most intense unlearning and relearning I've ever experienced, and I am so much better because of each and every one of you. Knowing all of you reminds me that it's impossible to collaborate in such meaningful ways unless your love for one another extends beyond the professional realm. Kass, shea, Kelly, Cody, Cornelius, Lizzie, Paul, Britt, Tiffany, Jess, Dulce-Marie, Daniella, y'all are the most brilliant, revolutionary, loving, and joyful people I have ever met. I love y'all forever.

To my sis Nina, Alonso, Axel, and Viggo. My life changed when Axel walked into my classroom on the first day of fourth grade. I wouldn't have this opportunity today if not for you. Thank you for the chicken dinners, ice cream sandwiches, Halloween excursions, impromptu come- dy shows in your living room, and inviting me into your family.

To Mr. Laurence Tan. "Hit the jackpot" doesn't begin to convey how lucky I was to have you as a mentor when I was an in-service teacher. You showed me what is possible starting from day one. It's been a number of years since we were together in your classroom in Watts, but there is still so much of you in how I teach to this day. You showed me what can be possible in this work and to never doubt the impact we can have as teachers, especially when we refuse to confine ourselves to the classroom. You will always be Yoda to my padawan.

To Dr. Sara Kersey. I never thought my graduate school professor, advisor, and mentor would also become one of my dear friends. You are such a phenomenal teacher and all-around human. The love, patience, and understanding that you showed me starting on day one of school is a huge reason why I try to approach my students with so much com- passion. Thank you for having my back on my best and worst days.

To my found family. Alpacas, IG crew, and my SFS squad. I am one hundred percent positive that I have the best friends in the entire world, and I can't express how much y'all mean to me. Thank you for the laughs, the pep talks, and your friendship. Meg, Jack, Bryan, all I can say is that I love you so much and cool cool cool I'm definitely not crying you're crying.

To my ancestors: It has taken me a long time to connect to you and hear your voices. While my life has taken many different turns, and some have felt determined by chance, I have no doubt that I am where I'm meant to be, doing what I'm meant to be doing. I recognize the strength I draw coming from a line of ancestors who have been colonized, enslaved, and persecuted across continents for centuries. I would not be here today if not for your strength, resilience, power, and sacrifice.

To every student who has come through my classroom door (both in person and virtually) in Oakland, Los Angeles, and DC, I love y'all so much. I hope you never forget that once you're my student, you're always my student. You are the real change makers, and I cannot wait to see what impact you have on the world.

To the Popsnorkles, my mom and dad. You're simply the best. Thank you for your unconditional love and support for all these years.

→

Acknowledgments

I have so many "isms" of yours that I've drawn on during my years of
teaching, and I'm always excited to pass on your wisdom to my students. Not only do I hope to make you two proud, but I am also SO
proud to be your daughter. I couldn't ask for better parents, and I love
you so much.

# INTRODUCTION

## YOU ARE NOT ALONE

> [T]he more radical the person is, the more fully he or she enters into reality so that, knowing it better, he or she can transform it. This individual is not afraid to confront, to listen, to see the world unveiled. This person is not afraid to meet the people or to enter into a dialogue with them. This person does not consider himself or herself the proprietor of history or of all people, or the liberator of the oppressed; but he or she does commit himself or herself, within history, to fight at their side.
>
> —PAULO FREIRE, *Pedagogy of the Oppressed*

**THERE ARE A LOT OF THINGS** people don't tell you when you write a book. When I first embarked on this project almost two years ago, the world was a different place, and I was a different person. No one tells you how much you will change, evolve, learn, and unlearn throughout the process. As I look through my earliest chapter drafts, I sometimes struggle to recognize the person who wrote those words. Many of my earlier thoughts and ideas are no longer my truth, nor do they apply to the future ahead. Even as I sit here proofreading my final draft, I caught half a dozen instances of ableist language that I did not have the lens to identify when I began writing two years ago. I wonder what else I will have learned and unlearned by the time I hold the finished book in my hands.

Things have changed since I started writing.

When I started writing this book, students were still gathering in classrooms. Teachers were able to give high fives as the school day began, and children could crowd together and play tag at recess. In March 2020, everything changed. More than half a million lives have been lost in the United States due to COVID-19, and nearly two million around the world. By the time this book is published, who knows how many more will no longer be with us. In the past months, video footage of Ahmaud Arbery being killed by a group of white men while jogging surfaced online. A Black woman and EMT named Breonna Taylor was shot and killed in her own home by police officers. The world watched a policeman suffocate George Floyd for nearly nine minutes as he lay on the ground gasping, "I can't breathe." The deaths of Black trans men and women continue to be ignored by the mainstream media. We've watched a mob attempt an insurrection on the United States Capitol, with people proudly sporting shirts with antisemitic propaganda. As I scramble to finish the final copyedits of this book, six Asian women were brutally murdered in Atlanta. These murders are following the attacks of numerous Asians and Asian Americans, many of them elderly, throughout this country. According to a study from California State University, San Bernardino, anti-Asian hate crimes have jumped 150 percent. This is the world our children and students are living in and watching unfold every day. How will we respond to them, hold space for them, and help them to dream of something better than what's on the screen in front of them?

My parents always told me to hope for the best and prepare for the worst.

As a child, I rolled my eyes because this seemed to be just another idiom they would toss out whenever I was struggling with an endeavor. However, now as an adult and having spent over a decade in the classroom, I've come to see the weight and wisdom of my parents' words.

My own racial and cultural identity and upbringing have largely shaped my approach to teaching, and what it means to be an aspiring antibias, antiracist, culturally responsive educator. I was born in South Korea and was adopted by a white-presenting, Ashkenazi Jewish family in Washington, DC. I spent my entire childhood at a prestigious prep school close to my home. I was challenged academically and learned many skills that would benefit me throughout college and graduate school. However, I grew up with a very narrow idea of what it means to be successful, and how success should be measured.

Aside from a few typical years of teenage angst in high school, I've always had a strong relationship with my parents. My parents were taught to not see race, and that it was best to try to ignore racialized identity in order to treat everyone equally. As a little kid, my parents read me picture books about adoption, and I have memories of demanding my parents tell me about the day I arrived as a bedtime story. On one occasion, my parents sent me to a Korean cultural camp for adoptees, which made a less than lasting impression. My dad tells the story of driving me and a few other kids to school one morning in our neighborhood carpool, and I announced to the car, "I'm Korean!" The other kids responded, "Well I'm Korean too!" "Yeah me too!" which my father found extremely humorous because all the other children were white. Aside from these small moments, my race and ethnicity as a Korean Asian American were rarely mentioned growing up. When you're a person of color raised in an environment where people claim to not see race and you grow up assuming that everyone is treated equally regardless of their race, it's difficult to "prepare for the worst," because you have no idea how harsh the world can be. To the readers who are opening this book and believe they do not "see color," I want you to know that I love my appearance and identity as an Asian American woman. When you claim to not see race, you are saying that you do not see or acknowledge personal identifiers that I love. You are viewing me through a lens of how you want to see me, rather than how I see myself.

     Rather than recite all of the experiences I've had with racism, antisemitism, and xenophobia, I wish to focus more energy on healing myself. Despite my struggle to define my identity when I was younger, I now come to view this duality as a gift. I recognize that my identity and my upbringing have put me in the unique position to be able to navigate spaces held by people of color, as well as those occupied by whiteness. As an East Asian American woman, I know that people may look at me and buy into the problematic model minority myth. It is unlikely that I will be accused of being angry, sassy, or aggressive when I speak out on issues of racial inequality. This is a privilege that I have been granted and hold myself accountable to spend it every day of my life.

     The purpose of divulging my experiences is to explain that, throughout my childhood, I felt like I was often navigating this alone. I often wonder how this journey would have been different if the adults in my life had made space for me to talk about the issues I was facing, rather than assume I was fine because I appeared to be handling things OK. It's the silence that speaks volumes. Whether it's a predominantly white school or a school that mainly serves students of color, the impact of racial and socioeconomic inequity reverberates in every community. We can continue to sit comfortably in that silence and maintain the status quo, or we can begin the conversations that allow students to feel seen and heard, and to participate in dismantling oppressive systems. The conversations, topics, and lessons I present in this book most likely dramatically deviate from your own educational experiences, as well as traditional educational pedagogy. However, claiming "This is how things have always been done" doesn't mean certain practices should be perpetuated. Deviating from the norm can be intimidating, but at the end of the day, we're here to meet the needs of our students rather than center our own comfort.

All students deserve a structured environment where they can feel safe to ask questions, express themselves, and share aspects of their identity. But to many educators, it feels as though we're navigating through a minefield in the dark. There is an urgency to invite students to share their lives and experiences in the classroom, and often their stories are intertwined with structures of systemic racism, classism, homophobia, and neurotypical standards. But if so many of us have been raised to pretend to not see race, confronting our own discomfort can often be the largest obstacle we face in cultivating an antibias antiracist classroom. So what can we do? We can take steps to set ourselves up for success, while also preparing ourselves for mistakes that will be made along the way.

I have had the opportunity to speak and work with teachers throughout the United States over the past few years, and two trends stand out: One is the desire of teachers to address current events, politics, race, and social justice issues in the classroom, and the other is the climate of fear surrounding it. The second is a fear that educators have expressed about doing this very thing. I've heard countless worries about the lack of support from administration, parents and caregivers lashing out, and feeling unequipped to facilitate these conversations. The goal of this book is to be transparent about the challenges that educators committed to antibias and antiracism face every day, and to provide concrete strategies to overcome some of the barriers that prevent us from engaging in this work.

While I recognize that my experience in the classroom has largely been successful due to the support of my community, not all teachers work in schools that accept this type of work. To be mindful of this reality, I have sought out the perspectives of teachers and administrators across the country to shed light on strategies that have been successful in diverse, homogenous, conservative, liberal, urban, and rural schools. My hope is that any educator will be able to pick up this book and identify a strategy they feel could be implemented or adapted to fit their own needs.

# Let's Get on the Same Page

In each chapter, you'll see some repetitive language, and it's important to get on the same page before we begin.

I describe both *race* and *gender* as social constructions, meaning these ideas were created by people, for specific purposes and categorization. There is no biological basis for race. *Gender*, *sex*, and *sexuality* are all different words with different meanings. Gender reflects the cultural norms and expectations of a society based on biological sex, while sexuality refers to one's sexual orientation. The concepts of both race and gender are also proven to be socially constructed ideas because they differ depending on cultural context (for example, when I received a fellowship to study in South Africa, I quickly learned that certain East Asian groups are considered "white"). For the purpose of this book, examples are contextualized within United States history and culture. Additionally, there are many disagreements about what constitutes *racism*. I lean toward the definition that racism is the product of power and prejudice. Racism is also multifaceted, and exists on individual, interpersonal, institutional, and structural levels. While it's easy to point out a racist in a white hood and robe, we must pay attention to how our individual actions and beliefs uphold racial inequities. In the Point Made Learning documentary *"I'm Not Racist . . . Am I?"* a group of students and their facilitator note that even if all of the overtly racist people in the country were shot into outer space, we would still exist in a racist society due to the presence of institutional and structural racism within every industry. Whenever any person reinforces white dominant culture or values, this perpetuates racism. As activist Angela Davis reminds us, "In a racist society it is not enough to be non-racist, we must be anti-racist." It is simply not enough to excuse ourselves from this work because we see ourselves as a good, nonracist person. It requires a constant practice of taking action to dismantle white supremacy and pushing back against white dominant culture and anti-Blackness.

>> When I talk about *race*, this is a socially constructed hierarchy based on power and prejudice, with whiteness perched at the very top.

>> While there is often disagreement about whether BIPOC can be racist, it is important to remember that everyone, regardless of their identity, is capable of colorism, bigotry, and holding biased beliefs.

» When I talk about *gender*, this is also a socially constructed idea, and is not meant to be confused with *sex*. There is also nuance between *gender identity* (how one identifies their gender) and *gender expression* (how one outwardly expresses themselves).

» You'll also see the acronym *ABAR*, which stands for antibias antiracist. ABAR is rooted in action by identifying our biases in order to dismantle white supremacist beliefs, values, and culture.

» I also use the term *BIPOC*, which stands for Black, Indigenous, people of color. However, this should not be used as an umbrella term when specifically identifying a community. For example, we must name that Black students are disproportionately suspended in schools and face harsher disciplinary actions compared to white students, rather than BIPOC students.

» BIPOC and nonwhite are not synonymous. For example, Ashkenazi Jews whose descendants are of Eastern European roots are not considered white (especially in the eyes of white supremacists) but are not considered people of color.

# What You'll Find in This Book

Teachers are notorious self-critics. Every day, we are expected to perform miracles with limited resources, time, and too often, support. In order for us to make progress in this work, it is important to be vulnerable and transparent. The barriers I address in this book were chosen based on feedback from educators all over the United States when asked, "What prevents you from pursuing social justice in your classroom?" You will read stories from educators, administrators, and family members, many of whom are struggling with the same questions and challenges you are currently facing. These include

» How do I get started if I'm new to ABAR work?

» There are so many things I need to get through in a school day. How can I make time for ABAR work?

>> How can I hold space for difficult conversations in my class?

>> Parents and caregivers have a lot of strong feelings about ABAR work. How can I work with them?

>> My administration seems reluctant when it comes to ABAR in the classroom. How can I convince them to support this work?

>> What does ABAR look like if all or most of my students are white?

>> What does developmentally appropriate ABAR look like for younger students?

>> What does ABAR look like if I teach STEM subjects?

So, what will this work look like in practice? Each chapter is organized in a similar format and provides a framework for tackling each barrier from a proactive stance.

# Setting Yourself Up for Success

In a tribute to my parents' words of wisdom, this section will help you hope for the best and plan for the worst through proactive strategies that should be set up before you even begin teaching. While I can only speak from my experiences in the classroom through my own personal lens, it is important to me that a variety of perspectives are represented. For example, if you're a STEM educator wondering how to incorporate ABAR into your work, I can share my experiences, but it will also be helpful to hear the successes of other STEM teachers, and learn from the resources that have supported their work. You'll also hear from a number of educators, administrators, and family members from different schools and communities who are committed to finding ways to create sustainable cultures around ABAR and culturally responsive teaching.

A huge key to success in this work is the ability to invite in and respect different perspectives, both with students and adults. My hope in bringing in a diverse variety of voices is to help educators understand where families, administrators, and colleagues are coming from.

The key is to remain solutions-oriented and identify the root cause of concerns in order to best address them.

# Taking Action in the Classroom

I have a strong dislike for educator books or trainings that live solely in the abstract. When I read a teaching book or attend a professional development session, I want to be able to walk away with something concrete that I can implement right away. In this section, you'll find sample lessons, conversation starters, anchor charts, communication templates, student samples, and real conversations that have occurred in classrooms.

# Creating a Sustainable Practice

As often as we ask our students to reflect upon what they've learned, are we creating space to ask ourselves important questions? How did this strategy go? What parts were successful? What lesson can we take into a future interaction? Teachers must be able to identify what is working, and what isn't, in order to avoid placing energy into impractical and unsustainable habits. Sometimes this may be a personal reflection, a class or family survey, or an observation of the classroom climate and culture.

There is no "one and done" lesson or book when it comes to social justice and culturally reflective teaching. This book is meant to help educators break habits that are holding them back from this work, as well as build positive, sustainable teaching for the future. Once you've found success in one lesson or unit, it's important to identify what worked, and what needs to be adapted for the long term. This section also includes additional resources, organizations, books, and trainings that will help educators build their practice over time.

One of my former school's operating norms for staff is "Use your airplane mask," meaning you have to be able to take care of yourself before you can take care of others (especially children!). Teaching is a marathon, not a sprint. When approximately half of teachers quit before spending five years in the classroom, self-care and burnout awareness are crucial. The nature of ABAR work can deplete not only your energy, but also your emotional capacity. It can often be a way to invigorate and energize teachers, but it can be extremely taxing when you don't advocate for your own well-being along the way.

As intimidating as this work may seem to those just getting started, the consequence of not talking about ABAR, equity, and inclusion in schools is far more severe. No one is born knowing how to be an active and engaged citizen. This is something we have to learn, and this is where schools and educators have a responsibility to ensure that students understand how our society operates, and how to communicate with people across the political and cultural spectrum. At the end of the day, we cannot fix problems we do not talk about, or that we cannot name. We can't hope to eradicate systemic racism if we don't understand race. We can't bridge political polarization if we don't teach our children to seek to understand, rather than argue to win. Our personal discomfort as educators cannot become barriers that prevent us from creating brave spaces for our students.

Before you dive into this book, I also want to own that I am a biased, imperfect, evolving individual. My identity and positionality have shaped my experiences and the way I see the world, and despite being in this field for some time, I am still incredibly ignorant. I am sure that for some readers, this book will fall short. Please know that I truly believe that the more I become aware of my limitations and the more I learn, the better I can do. If I get something wrong, I invite you to call me in.

I warn you now that there is no "one size fits all" when it comes to ABAR work. For some schools, this might look like encouraging your students to give up or spend their privilege and power to ensure equity and access for others, and in other schools it might look like helping your students use their own voices to advocate for themselves and their communities. The strategies in this book may not work for everyone, but my hope is that they empower educators to take the first step toward reimagining the possibilities of how ABAR can transform schools and the world at large. There will be moments of discomfort. You will be questioned, others might push back, and there will be moments when you feel isolated in this work, but at the end of the day, I promise you that you are not alone.

It's been months since schools moved away from brick-and-mortar buildings and into virtual spaces. While some have returned to classrooms, nearly every student in the United States has been impacted by distance schooling or crisis schooling. We do not know when students and teachers will be able to gather and co-create a physical learning community. Everywhere you look, we are experiencing collective trauma as our country burns.

I try to keep reminding myself that fire can be cleansing. Fire can be used to purify and start over. We knew that inequities were prevalent in education before the pandemic began, and distance schooling has only exacerbated these injustices. The number one request I have of educators as we face an uncertain future is this: When we experience trauma, it is in our nature to crave what is comfortable and familiar. We have to remember that not only are students experiencing and processing trauma, but so are educators and caregivers. Where we are getting it wrong is that we're expecting teachers to go back to the comfortable and easy places when we know these practices weren't benefiting students in the first place. When we resort to traditional methods because they're familiar yet harmful, this is engaging in a trauma response.

However, we're not interested in returning to normal. As my friends and colleagues Kass and Cornelius Minor have said, "Normal left too many of us in the margins." While nostalgia and comfort keep calling us back, remember that this is a truly unique opportunity to build something better for our children, our schools, and ourselves. This is our opportunity to reinvent normal and dismantle oppressive systems that we always knew existed, but have a new light shed upon them. Antibias and antiracist education is not optional. Educators, parents, and caregivers need to commit themselves to ensuring that their non-Black children will not endanger the lives of their Black peers. All people need to educate themselves about the insidious nature of white supremacy, and correct the imbalance that places Black, Brown, disabled, under-resourced, immigrant, and LGBTQ+ lives on a lesser plane than others. It is not enough to proclaim your hatred of injustice, but rather ask how you are showing love to your most marginalized students. The world we seek to build has never existed, but we must be courageous, remind ourselves that what is right is often not what is easy, and continue to dream. Amid the chaos, our path ahead is clear. This is our chance to dream big and build something better.

START HERE START NOW

# How Do I Get Started If I'm New to ABAR Work?

START
HERE

**I'M AN AVID HORROR MOVIE FAN.** My friends find it simultaneously amusing and strange that my idea of a relaxing evening is scrolling through streaming apps trying to find a horror film that I haven't seen. Not long ago, a friend and I were talking about an upcoming movie and he asked me, "What do you think makes people feel scared?"

As a horror enthusiast, I've always been fascinated by this question and I've come to believe that fear comes from a lack of control (aside from the amygdala in our brain). It's not about not knowing the outcome of a situation. It's the inability to predict how, what, or when something is going to happen. Take the example of riding a roller coaster. You know it's going to drop. You know that slow ride up the hill is going to make your heart race. Even though you know exactly what's going to happen, the fear comes from not having any control over the impending drop. For some people, this fear is thrilling and exciting, and for others, their worst nightmare is a trip to Six Flags.

For educators who are new to antibias and antiracist (ABAR) work, there may be a myriad of worries coming from different directions. The good news is that you do not have to take on everything at once. We can start to make progress by confronting what makes us nervous and be proactive by setting ourselves up for success. I believe the insecurities that can hold educators back stem from the same place—the unpredictability of classroom conversations, recognizing your own ignorance, the fear of making mistakes or not knowing enough, and not knowing how students, caregivers, and administrators might react. Over the past few years, I've spoken to hundreds of teachers about why they're not engaging with their students in conversations surrounding ABAR issues. Given the history of racial injustice and social inequality in the United States, as well as events unfolding every day, it's extremely hard to ignore these topics. The majority express their desire to engage but avoid ABAR topics because they're afraid of saying the wrong thing. In these moments, we must remember that too much is at risk to avoid this work, and centering our own comfort is a reflection of the privilege we hold.

When educators wonder how they can work around defensive caregivers and unsupportive administrators, some fear being accused of pushing a political agenda on students, and others feel completely overwhelmed by finding resources, self-educating, and educating their students. Despite having read up on critical race theory and culturally responsive practices, they have no idea what concrete steps to take in order to actively engage with students or write a lesson plan.

If any of these concerns resonate with you, rest assured that you are not alone. Taking the first step to address issues around ABAR can be intimidating. Before you begin, it helps to accept that mistakes will be made. Sometimes the lessons and conversations with students will be complicated and messy, and you should get comfortable saying, "That's a good question, I don't know!" To build a student-centered community of learners, educators have to engage in deep self-reflection and identity work, de-center themselves, and relinquish some control of their classroom. While this may sound scary, it's possible to set yourself up with strategic, proactive choices.

# Setting Yourself Up for Success: Develop a Lens for Antibias Practices, and Don't Reinvent the Wheel

Every educator I interviewed for this book was asked the same question: What advice would you give to a teacher just starting out with developing their ABAR lens and practice? Nearly everyone gave a variation of the same response: You have to start with yourself. An ABAR teaching practice does not solely exist between the time the school bell rings and the time students are dismissed. While I have been engaged in this work for a number of years, I'm constantly reading and listening to people who have lived experiences different from my own. Like most folks, I sometimes feel uncomfortable when presented with a perspective that pushes against a preconceived notion, but I try to view these moments as opportunities to grow and learn. Accept that ABAR work is open-ended and abstract. Because our learning and comfort exist on a spectrum, there is no finish line to cross.

## Get to Know Yourself

If you've never reflected on your identity and experiences, it is crucial that you begin before engaging in ABAR work with students. You cannot expect or ask your students to share parts of themselves that you yourself have not unpacked. Have you spent time reflecting on the intersections of your own identity? How do you experience privilege and oppression? How did your identity impact your own experience as a student? It's difficult to help guide students to develop their personal identities or address their biases if you're not familiar with your own.

The three images in Figures 1–1a, 1–1b, and 1–1c are personal identity maps I created based on the work of Kimberlé Crenshaw, a Black female legal scholar and activist who coined the term *intersectionality*. The term appeared in the *Oxford Dictionary of Human Geography* in 2013, defined as "The interconnected nature of social categorizations such as race, class, and gender as they apply to a given individual or group, regarded as creating overlapping and interdependent systems of discrimination or disadvantage" (Castree, Kitchin, and Rogers 2013). In these identity maps, I've shown my personal identity markers (race, ethnicity, gender, religion, and so on), and highlighted the parts of my identity that are important to me, contrasted with the parts of my identity that I felt were the most validated by my teachers and schools.

As you can see in the last map, the parts of my identity that were the most validated did not overlap with the parts of me that I deem to be the most important. Additionally, these specific social identity markers are also where I hold the most privilege (when I say *privilege*, I think about the ways in which I'm set up to thrive in our society due to my social identities). Processes like these have helped me to reflect upon the ways in which I see and value my students in class, as well as where I might hold biases or preferences, and how I can become more aware in order to dismantle them.

Try creating your own identity map. Use the template in Figure 1–2. While it certainly doesn't include all possible identity markers, it's a good place to start.

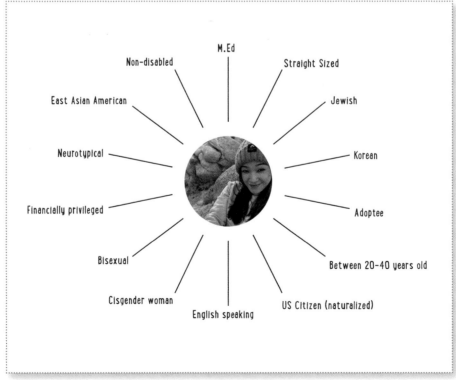

FIGURE 1–1A Personal Identity Map

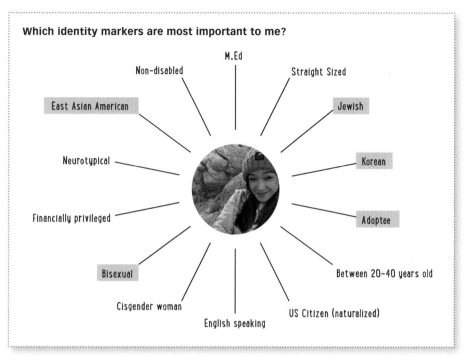

FIGURE 1–1B Personal Identity Map with Most Important Characteristics Highlighted

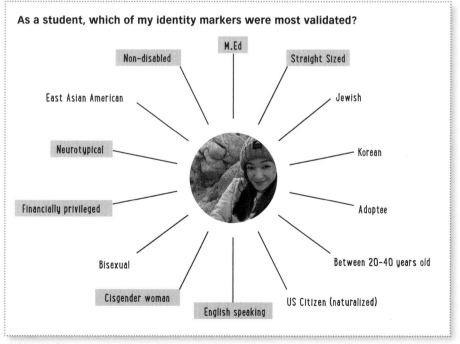

FIGURE 1–1C Personal Identity Map with Characteristics Validated in School

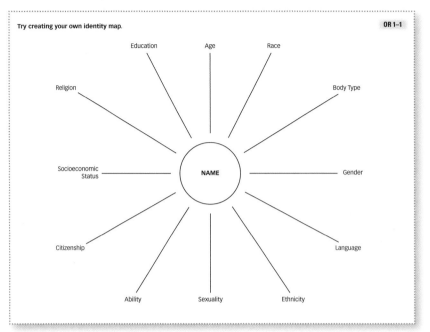

FIGURE 1–2 Identity Map Template

## Practice Viewing Students, Families, and Communities Through an Asset Lens

Looking back at my own journey, I cringe when I think about how I used to proudly share that I taught in a Title-1 school. There are so many words used to describe students and schools, like *urban* and *disadvantaged*, that carry so much negative weight, yet educators use them to convey defining characteristics of their environments. Think about the language you use when you refer to your students and ask yourself whether you use phrases that focus on what they can do as opposed to what they can't. For example, the label *English Language Learner* views the student through a deficit lens because they are not fully fluent in English, while an asset lens may view the student as an *emerging bilingual*, which celebrates their access to two languages. Education researcher and teacher Gloria Ladson-Billings wrote about the "education debt," which focuses on inequitable systems, as opposed to the "achievement gap," which blames students for their perceived lack of success (Ladson-Billings 2006). While new ABAR terminology is constantly becoming more visible in mainstream spaces, I personally use social media to keep up to date, especially by learning from people who have very different identities than my own.

Once you know who your students are, how are you continuing to educate yourself about their identities and backgrounds? Understanding the broader social and political contexts that have shaped students' identities is also an integral part of community building. I recently coached a teacher who was concerned about supporting her Southeast Asian students. Together we discussed the impact of US participation in the Vietnam War (this history is almost always told from the US perspective), but this time from the voices of Vietnamese scholars and writers. We also studied postwar immigrants' stories and the impact of immigration policies on the community. To be culturally responsive, you have to recognize and understand the cultures your students are coming from.

## Think of Yourself as a Community Educator

Dr. Sara Kersey (she/her), who teaches and advises graduate students in UCLA's Teacher Education Program, asks her cohort to shift their lens from classroom teachers to community educators and to think about how teachers participate as community members in places where they teach. Dr. Kersey (2019) emphasizes the importance of viewing students, families, and communities through an asset lens. Many teachers do not live in the neighborhoods where they teach due to biases they hold about the communities, and despite working in these schools week after week, they remain outsiders.

So how can teachers think of themselves as community educators if we do not live where we teach? First and foremost, Kersey suggests we spend time in the areas around our school, even if we do not live there. "Are you aware of local shops, restaurants, and community spaces? Do you know where your students spend time outside of school? When you ask them about what they do in their free time, do you listen without judgment? Before the school year begins, try to go out and familiarize yourself with the community around your school. Don't just drive around as an observer but try to engage with the people you encounter. Ask what they love about their neighborhood, how long they've lived there, and try to listen and learn about the wealth of the community and the resources that exist."

# Taking Action in the Classroom: Create Space for Students' Identities with Community-Building Activities

A practical way to get started is to plan community-building activities that allow space for students' identities. We want students to be able to share their thoughts and feelings about who they are—similarities, differences, and personal experiences. The beginning of the year is the best time for both teachers and students to practice their fluency when describing personal feelings, experiences, and opinions. It will help establish a strong foundation for the year. However, you'll want to revisit community-building activities throughout the year.

## "I Am From" Poems

One community-building activity that invites students to share about themselves and also gives insight into their lives outside of school is an "I Am From" poem. This activity is inspired by George Ella Lyon's poem "Where I'm From" (1993). Figure 1–3 is an example of one student's poem.

Start with the organizer in Figure 1–4. Use it to model how students can think about and describe the uniqueness of their homes, families, and identities. You can brainstorm as a class

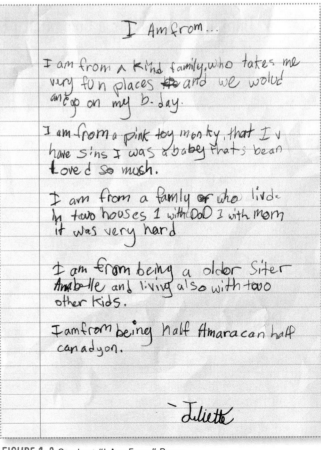

FIGURE 1–3 Student "I Am From" Poem

NAME: _____ OR 1–2

### "I Am From" Poem Organizer
(Think about your FIVE SENSES! What do you SEE, HEAR, SMELL, TASTE, and FEEL?)

| Favorite things in your home | What does your home look like? |
|---|---|
| Your family members (names, nicknames) | Favorite foods (and foods you eat on special occasions) |
| Family traditions | Things that people in your family always say to you |

© 2021 by Liz Kleinroth, from *Start Here, Start Now*. Portsmouth, NH: Heinemann.

## FIGURE 1–4
### "I Am From" Planning Organizer

| Countries, states, or cities where your family is from | Languages spoken in your family (words/phrases your family says to each other in your language) |
|---|---|
| Where do you keep important things in your home? | Things, people, or places you see in your neighborhood |
| Favorite places you go with your family | Your hobbies, and what you like to do in your free time |

© 2021 by Liz Kleinroth, from *Start Here, Start Now*. Portsmouth, NH: Heinemann.

one prompt at a time or allow students to go at their own pace by giving them the organizer (either online or a hard copy). I ask quick finishers to reread and add sensory details to bring their descriptions to life, or specific moments in time. For example, if I wrote, "I am from my pet bunny," I can add, "I am from my pet bunny *who is soft, fluffy, and twitches her nose.*"

With younger students, slow down the process; it might take a few days to teach them how to write "I Am From" poems. Start by showing examples (use your poem!) and reading them aloud. Then brainstorm ideas. You might have students turn and talk as a way to rehearse their thinking. Once students understand what they'll be working on, use an organizer that breaks down the sections of the poem. Use the organizer in Figure 1–5 or change it to fit the needs of your students. Remember, this activity can be tailored to your students based on what they are comfortable sharing, and there's no one correct way to craft this poem.

If you're asking your students to be vulnerable with you and their classmates, it's important to remember that trust and respect go both ways. I strongly believe that educators have to work consistently to humanize themselves to their students, and must view themselves as partners, not leaders, in this work. Modeling how to brainstorm ideas for this poem is an effective way for me to share aspects of my childhood, interests, and personal experiences. See Figure 1–6 for my "I Am From" poem.

As I drafted and modeled the writing process for this poem, different parts of my story resonated with my students. Some were delighted to learn that I had a stuffed animal that I loved, and a few related to not physically resembling members of their own families. "I Am From" poems can be used in different ways and at different times—as beginning of the year introductions, end of the year reflections, poetry unit extensions, and as tools to develop writing through elaborative details and figurative language.

OR 1–3

I am _____
(Your name)

I am from _____
(What do you like doing? What are you good at?)

I am from _____
(People who are important to you)

I am from _____
(Family traditions)

I am from _____
(Favorite foods or special foods you like from home)

I am a _____
(What do you look like?)

I am from _____
(Important events in your life)

I am from _____
(Your favorite books, movies, shows)

I am from _____
(Where you live)

I am _____
(Your name)

© 2021 by Liz Kleinrock, from *Start Here, Start Now*. Portsmouth, NH: Heinemann.

**FIGURE 1–5**
"I Am From" Organizer
for Younger Students

Ms. Liz

### I AM FROM

I am from a yellow house on a quiet street, where the snow never gets plowed in the winter.

I am from a stuffed animal monkey that has been loved so much for so long, its fur is falling out and its eyes have become scratched and worn.

I am from hot porridge on bad days, and waffle breakfasts on weekend mornings.

I am from a family full of love, even though my parents and I do not look alike.

I am from a lamp shaped like a goose, magical night lights, and checking for aliens under the bed.

I am from Friday night Shabbat dinners, and watching TV sandwiched between my parents on the couch.

I am from Chinese food and horror movie marathons with friends, and hiding under the covers.

I am from merry-go-rounds of flying horses, capturing rings, and salt water taffy.

I am from, "Work hard, play hard," and, "Don't sweat the small stuff."

I am from the life of a transplant, moving from the east to the west coast.

I am from places where I'm not sure if I belong.

**FIGURE 1–6**
My "I Am From" Poem

## Identity Maps

After creating and reflecting on your identity map, have students create their own. Use the template in Figure 1–7 or create your own.

It can be helpful for students to make identity maps at the beginning and end of the year. For younger students, it's a tremendous opportunity for them to see their writing progress side by side. For all students, it's an opportunity to reflect on how much they've changed in a year and recognize their own growth and self-understanding. Figures 1–8a and 1–8b show third grader David's identity maps from the beginning and end of the year.

Identity maps can also be created in different ways, and students do not have to be restricted to a particular design or layout. For students who love to draw or enjoy graphic novels, identity one-pagers

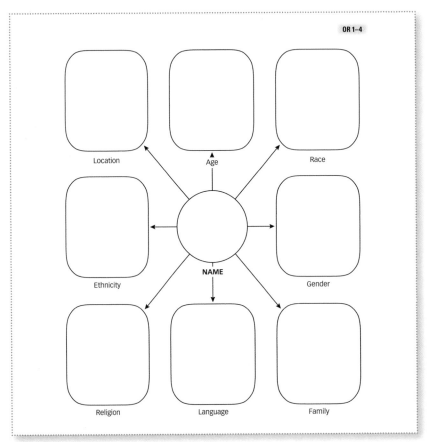

FIGURE 1–7 Identity Map II Template

like the one in Figure 1–9 are another way to share about themselves or their families. In this activity, students can choose to illustrate and

**FIGURES 1–8A AND 1–8B**
A Student's Beginning and End of the Year Identity Map

FIGURE 1-9 A Student's Identity One-Pager About Their Parent

represent important parts of themselves or a family member and tell their life story through images.

## Bio Bag Reveals

One of my favorite identity and community-building activities is to use bio bags. Each student receives a paper bag, and on the outside writes the visible parts of their identity. On the inside, students place cards with parts of their identity that are visible when you get to know them, or when they choose to share. This helps remind students and teachers that only some parts of ourselves are visible to others, and that we should be careful when making assumptions about others. Again, model by making your own and decide the best way for students to share—during class meeting times, in small groups, or in partnerships. Figure 1–10 shows Sofia's bio bag. On the bio bag, Sofia identifies as an athlete and a reader. Inside the bag, Sofia identifies as "Jewish," "I make my own comic book," and "likes to identify as a boy."

## Make Time and Space for Student Reflection and Emotional Processing

As classroom teachers, we are responsible for the social and emotional health and well-being of our students. Lessons around ABAR topics can be emotionally taxing for both young people and adults. Some ideas

**FIGURE 1–10**
A Student's Bio Bag Reveal

may be easy to process, while others may require days or weeks to grapple with and understand.

Sometimes when I'm working through my emotions or learning about an upsetting event, it helps to talk about how I'm feeling. Sometimes I like to journal. Sometimes I need to shut down and take a break and come back to it later. From my own self-understanding, I know it's important to create multiple ways for students to reflect and process.

Sometimes we're aware of how a conversation makes us feel in the moment, and at other times we feel the weight hours or days later. When we ask students to reflect on or process emotions and events, there should be no time limits. Give students choices about how and when they reflect. The responses in Figures 1–11 through 1–13 came from third- and fourth-grade students after they were asked questions about privilege, race, and age. Oftentimes the best way to gauge your students' emotional state is simply to ask, "How did learning about _____ make you feel?" Here are some additional reflection prompts:

» Did you feel any personal connection to what we learned about today? If so, what did you connect to?

» What questions do you still have about this topic?

» On a scale of 1–10, how challenging was it to learn about this topic and why?

FIGURES 1–11A AND 1–11B Student Responses to the Question: "What would you say to adults who think you're too young to learn about current events?"

We can think the same way you do.

I would say I think wa are big enough to Learn about thes things becuase most problums are about hapening wher we live

I feel it is important to learn about. I also feel uncomfortable talking about race. But I feel students should learn about it to learn how to stop racism.

FIGURE 1–12 Student Reflection on Race

Some privileges I have are going to school and having enough money to sustain my family and having a working body and have both of my parents alive and not being discriminated by what color skin I was BORN with. I finally notice that I am very lucky to be who I am and all of these privileges I was born with.

FIGURE 1–13 Student Reflection on Privilege

>> Are there any ideas connected to this topic that you'd also like to learn about?

>> As your teacher, how can I support your learning about this topic?

## Discover What Students Already Know

It's difficult to know what to teach unless you understand what your students already know. It's also hard to track your students' understandings unless you have some baseline data for comparison (especially if you teach in a school where data and testing are the be-all and end-all). During the first few weeks of school, and again at the end of the year, I ask my students to answer a series of questions that reflect their understanding of terms and concepts such as *race*, *stereotyping*, *equality*, and *diversity*. Not only do these surveys show what my students know or don't know, but they also identify any misconceptions the students may have. Figure 1–14 shows a variety of questions that educators can use to identify prior knowledge and misconceptions.

One of the most rewarding parts of committing to ABAR work in the classroom is seeing how your students' understanding grows as you dig deeper into these conversations and lessons. Asking students to answer these questions at the beginning and near the end of the year allows you to quickly obtain information about how your students have grown and address any misconceptions that may still exist. Figures 1–15 and 1–16 show one

FIGURE 1-14 Social Justice Student Survey Template

student's responses in August and May. Notice the reluctant and blank responses in August compared to the more confident and extensive way the student responds at the end of the school year.

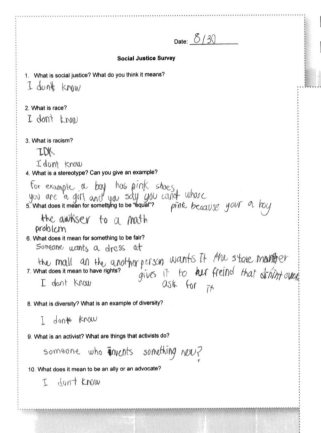

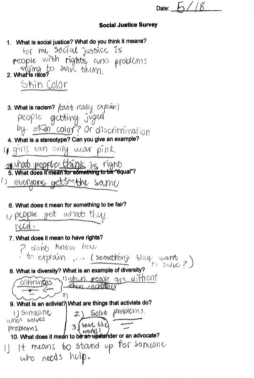

FIGURE 1–15 Social Justice Student Survey August

FIGURE 1–16 Social Justice Student Survey May

# Creating a Sustainable Practice

Developing an ABAR practice is a lifelong journey without a finish line. There's no list of boxes to check. It sounds daunting, but this also means that we can self-pace and monitor our progress. Even when units and lessons go beautifully, we are never done. There is always more to learn and unlearn. In any industry, but especially in education, it is dangerous when we get to a place where we think we've learned all there is to know. This is when we stop growing, and our students notice.

## How Do I Know If It's Working?

While there is no binder of answers or a script of how to talk to your students, there are questions that can help you assess your practice, build upon what is successful, and focus on areas of need.

>> How did students respond to the community-building activities? Which one should I repeat?

>> What did I learn about my students through the community-building activities?

>> What evidence do I have that students feel seen in my classroom?

>> Who speaks up the most? How are all students participating?

>> Which students did I spend the most time with this week? Did I praise or redirect certain students more than others? Are there any patterns?

>> Did I use deficit-based language to describe any of my students (even if it's internal self-talk)?

## Don't Reinvent the Wheel

While many educators new to ABAR work may feel lost when it comes to locating resources, it's important to know that you do not have to create everything from scratch. When I first entered the classroom, I felt there was a severe lack of books and resources for elementary classrooms, and I spent a lot of time modifying lessons that had been written for middle and high school students. These days, there is a myriad of fantastic ABAR material for all age groups, but some of the best resources aren't widely circulated.

### Organizations and Publications with Curriculum and Lessons:

>> Learning for Justice, www.learningforjustice.org

> Teaching Hard History, www.learningforjustice.org /frameworks/teaching-hard-history/american-slavery

» Facing History and Ourselves, www.facinghistory.org

» Rethinking Schools, https://rethinkingschools.org

» Zinn Education Project, www.zinnedproject.org

» Museum education websites:

> Smithsonian National Museum of African American History and Culture, https://nmaahc.si.edu

> Smithsonian Asian Pacific American Center, https://smithsonianapa.org

> Smithsonian National Museum of the American Indian, https://americanindian.si.edu/visit/washington/nnavm

> Wing Luke Museum, www.wingluke.org

> Museum of Tolerance, www.museumoftolerance.com

> US Holocaust Memorial Museum, www.ushmm.org

> Arab American National Museum, https://arabamerican museum.org

> The Mexican Museum, www.mexicanmuseum.org

> National Civil Rights Museum, www.civilrightsmuseum.org

» Lee and Low Books, www.leeandlow.com

## Additional Self-Education

» *Code Switch*, podcast created by NPR

» *Nice White Parents*, podcast created by Serial and the *New York Times*

» *Intersectionality Matters!*, podcast created by the African American Policy Forum

» *Good Ancestor Podcast*, created by Layla F. Saad

» *Asian Enough*, podcast created by the *Los Angeles Times*

» *Disability After Dark*, podcast created by Andrew Gurza

# How Can I Make Time for ABAR Work?

START HERE

**NOT LONG AGO,** I was on a call with a friend who had just started teaching at a new school because she and her partner moved out of state. She loved the autonomy she'd had at her last school. After interviewing at a few schools in her new city, she accepted a job at a school that appeared promising. Soon after she started, she found herself highly scrutinized by her new administration and colleagues. "I feel like every minute of the day is dictated for me," she said. "Everyone has to use the same curriculum and teach the same things at the same time. All the teachers on my team have been there longer than me and they insist we all read the same books. If your bulletin boards look different than everyone else's, teachers talk about you. I used to teach things like ethnic studies and do all these projects with my students. You can barely call this teaching. It's like reading a script written by someone else."

My friend is not the only teacher working in this type of environment. I know many educators who express the desire to engage in

ABAR work with their students but feel there is no time in an already packed schedule. Some share stories of being written up for failing to post the daily standards on the board. Others say they feel anxious from being monitored by administrators who walk into classrooms to see if everyone is teaching the same lesson at the same time. One teacher shared, "At my first school, I taught along with six other teachers on my team. If we didn't give a unit test all in the same day, an administrator would visit our room and we would get reprimanded. It would also be noted that we were 'uncooperative,' or 'weren't being a team player.' Strict pacing was a huge challenge. I could recognize that students needed more time on a topic but if my class averages were low, I'd be questioned if I taught the material. Creativity was stifled because people felt like those activities would take too many class periods." States either have their own standards or utilize Common Core State Standards. Some even have requirements of how many minutes should be spent teaching certain subjects each day.

I certainly don't want to speak for other teachers regarding pacing and scripted curricula. For many people, especially those who are new to teaching, designated lessons and agendas can help provide structure. However, when teachers are handed boxes of curriculum and a prescribed schedule with little room for flexibility or creativity, it can be challenging to determine when and how to incorporate subjects that don't fit into traditional subject blocks. It's demoralizing to feel like you don't have time to address ABAR work in your classroom, but there are ways to weave it into your mandated curriculum.

# Setting Yourself Up for Success: Viewing ABAR as a Lens for All Subjects

First and foremost, effective and meaningful ABAR work is neither an add-on to your curriculum nor a separate block on your agenda. If you walk into my classroom, you will not see "9:30–10:00 A.M.: Social Justice Time" written on the whiteboard schedule. Many teachers view ABAR work as an either/or option, as if they have to decide between science and social justice and can only teach one. When ABAR is truly part of your teaching philosophy and practice, it becomes a *lens* through which you can teach any and all subjects.

## Think About How ABAR Work Aligns with Your Curriculum and Standards

Dr. Sara Kersey (she/her) of UCLA's Teacher Education Program recounted working with novice teachers who were trying to integrate social justice topics but felt stifled by curriculum requirements. "It's vitally important to have strong knowledge of the standards because you can't adapt any curriculum until you know what the students are going to be held accountable to standards-wise" (2019). If sticking to the standards is a priority, get to know the standards at the grade level you teach, as well as the previous and upcoming grades.

Standards-aligned instruction can be interpreted in many ways. If your school requires that you visibly display the lesson plan standards, you need to know them well enough to explain how students will master them. For example, the California fourth-grade social studies standards focus heavily on state history, including immigration, Indigenous peoples, missions, and the Gold Rush. If you were to enter my classroom, you might see my students reading accounts of Chinese railroad workers, women, and formerly enslaved African Americans during the Gold Rush; writing comparative essays about immigration issues in the past and present; or reflecting on the impact of climate change on California's agricultural production and what we can do to combat the drought in our everyday lives.

If an administrator were to enter my classroom and saw my students working on any of these assignments, I would immediately be able to identify which standards were being addressed, and how students were independently practicing these skills. I could either show them a chart like the one in Figure 2–1 or I could explain what standards we are working on and how my students will meet those standards.

Becoming familiar with the standards and curriculum of your school or district allows you to plan backward and ahead. It also helps you identify areas to supplement or replace or that might require additional student resources. Ask yourself: Are certain standards and curricular units emphasized more than others? How can you organize your time to focus on the concepts your students need to explore the most? In Figure 2–2, I show you how I might think through curriculum requirements. I identify the subjects I have to teach and what I have to teach within each subject and consider the content with an ABAR lens.

You can start with one subject or work across subjects, as I did. It's also helpful to fill out the planner with a grade team or a PLC.

You can also organize ABAR work across multiple subjects under a common theme. When I was a second-grade teacher, one of my earliest units focused on gender stereotyping and representation. I based this unit on conflicts that cropped up between students making generalizations such as "Girls can't do that . . . " or "Boys aren't supposed to. . . . " After becoming thoroughly exasperated with the constant stereotyping in my class, I wanted to figure out a way to blend social–emotional learning with our academic subjects. Additionally, as my own awareness developed, I recognized the importance of including and elevating nonbinary and trans people, who had been left out by male–female stereotyping. How could I use the theme of gender stereotyping as a way to synthesize our math, reading, and writing lessons, and open our discussions up to the real world? Concepts taught in isolation are far less likely to stick, and I couldn't put every subject on hold in order to solve social problems.

FIGURE 2–1 Aligning Standards to Instruction Sample Chart

| State Standard | How My Students Will Meet the Standard |
| --- | --- |
| **NGSS Fourth-Grade Science Standard: 4-ESS3-2** Generate and compare multiple solutions to reduce the impacts of natural Earth processes on humans. | ▪ Students will develop background knowledge by studying Indigenous peoples and movements protecting the land and natural resources. ▪ Students will use background knowledge to collaborate and develop a solution to an environmental problem based on Indigenous practices, such as traditional burning. |
| **CCSS Fourth-Grade Reading: Informational Texts CCSS.ELA-LITERACY.RI.4.6** Compare and contrast a firsthand and secondhand account of the same event or topic; describe the differences in focus and the information provided. | ▪ Students will study multiple perspectives of activists in the Civil Rights Movement through resources such as newspaper articles, nonfiction picture and chapter books, and documentary interviews. |
| **CCSS Fourth-Grade Writing: CCSS.ELA-LITERACY.W.4.2.D** Use precise language and domain-specific vocabulary to inform about or explain the topic. | ▪ Students and teacher will co-create ABAR word wall as a living resource. Sample vocabulary words may include *equality, equity, justice, stereotype,* among others. ▪ Students will use specific ABAR terms when writing informational pieces and personal reflections. |

FIGURE 2–2 ABAR Curriculum and Standards Planner

| Subject | What do I *have* to do in order to do what I *want* to do? | How can I tackle this through an ABAR lens? | What/where can I supplement/ substitute? |
|---|---|---|---|
| **Reading** | I have to teach a unit on fairy tales that requires reading multiple versions of *Cinderella*. | ■ I can teach about gender norms and gendered language.<br>■ I can lead discussions about how fairy tales can impact our ideas of gender expectations. | ■ I can add to this unit by comparing and contrasting other fairy and folk tales that counter stereotypes of male saviorism and female competition. |
| **Writing** | I have to teach my students lessons on grammar and sentence structure. | ■ I can take time to learn about my students' backgrounds and make connections to their home languages.<br>■ I can commit to never shaming my students for mispronouncing words.<br>■ I can be aware of biases I may have toward students who are emerging bilinguals or who speak with an accent. | ■ I can teach about how letter-sound correspondence differs across languages.<br>■ I can teach about AAVE (African American Vernacular English) as its own language.<br>■ I can teach my students about code switching and how different contexts sometimes require different types of writing. |
| **Math** | I have to make sure my students demonstrate automaticity in solving single-digit multiplication problems. | ■ I can ask my students, "Did anyone solve this problem using a different strategy?" to show that there are many valid ways to problem solve other than the standard algorithm.<br>■ I can give my students ample thinking time and recognize that not all students enjoy participating by sharing their answers in front of the class. | ■ I can tie in real-world connections, such as everyday applications for multiplication, using topics like time and money. |

*(continues)*

FIGURE 2–2 ABAR Curriculum and Standards Planner *(continued)*

| Subject | What do I *have* to do in order to do what I *want* to do? | How can I tackle this through an ABAR lens? | What/where can I supplement/ substitute? |
|---|---|---|---|
| **Science** | I have to teach a series of isolated lessons and units that do not connect to one another but are parts of a large curriculum. | ■ I can model that this class is a place where mistakes are expected, inspected, and respected.<br>■ I can be intentional about defining new content vocabulary words rather than assuming background knowledge. | ■ I can take the time to understand the scope and sequence of the curriculum, in order to identify units that could be paired or re-situated throughout the year. For example, a stand-alone unit on waves and currents could be paired with a unit on climate and environmental change. |
| **Social Studies** | I have to teach social studies standards on European explorers. | ■ I can center the perspectives of Indigenous peoples and discuss the impact of colonization throughout history to the present day.<br>■ I can also teach about bias by analyzing texts by Western authors that teach explorer history. | ■ I can use the book *An Indigenous Peoples' History of the United States for Young People* by Roxanne Dunbar-Ortiz, adapted by Jean Mendoza and Debbie Reese, and *A Young People's History of the United States* by Howard Zinn, adapted by Rebecca Stefoff. |
| **Physical Education** | I have to conduct a physical fitness test with my students where they're required to participate in timed and measured activities such as running a mile and doing a certain number of push-ups. | ■ I can be aware if I hold fat-phobic beliefs as I discuss the concept of health with my students.<br>■ I can commit to avoiding gendered language, such as "Boys line up here," to create an inclusive space for students across the gender spectrum. | ■ I can use resources such as *The Body Issue* from ESPN to show diversity in the human form, and that there is no one-sized "healthy" body.<br>■ I can tie in social issues such as diet culture to build awareness around what we consume in the media and how it influences the way we think about ourselves. |

*(continues)*

FIGURE 2–2 ABAR Curriculum and Standards Planner *(continued)*

| Subject | What do I *have* to do in order to do what I *want* to do? | How can I tackle this through an ABAR lens? | What/where can I supplement/substitute? |
|---|---|---|---|
| Art | I have to teach about symmetry in art as well as drawing and painting techniques such as shading. | ■ I can create self-portrait assignments and talk about the beauty of our skin tones, and how to create them on paper.<br>■ I can make observations about students' artwork and ask questions, but avoid judgmental remarks like "This is so pretty!" | ■ I can unpack the term *masters* when describing white, Western male visual artists.<br>■ I can incorporate the work of artists of color and female artists such as Betye Saar, Ruth Asawa, and Augusta Savage.<br>■ I can focus on how art is used as a form of activism and protest. |

## Adopt a Critical Lens to Problematic Mandated Books

Many educators are concerned about being forced to teach books and curricula that perpetuate stereotypes or elevate white Eurocentric narratives and history. Sometimes they are ostracized by colleagues for speaking up. In these situations, teachers can refocus their lessons by adopting a critical lens, or by juxtaposing the required text or lesson with another. Dr. Kersey described one such situation with a novice teacher who was required to teach Mark Twain's *Adventures of Tom Sawyer*, but felt it was outdated, and wanted her fifth-grade students in Los Angeles to read more culturally responsive books.

> *First we had a conversation about the spaces where she feels like she could push against that text, even if she couldn't throw it out completely. So one of the things that I asked her was, if you can't throw it out altogether, how can you make it quick and over? I suggested that she get the excerpt that she has to read on an audio book and have her kids just listen to the text, but then pair the book with something more relevant and figure out how to do some comprehension work related to the problems involved in the text. Another direction to go in was to have her students critically examine the themes in the book. Not just*

*understanding the who, what, where, and when, but dig into the problematic notions of gender and race.*

Dr. Kersey suggests that if you're required to teach a book like *The Adventures of Tom Sawyer,* do it from a perspective that will feel more meaningful and relevant to your students. In Figure 2–3, I share a few of her examples along with options she offers to both critique and focus on the themes of the text. I also note how teaching with an ABAR lens meets the standards.

FIGURE 2–3 Teaching Mandated Texts Through an ABAR Lens

| Mandated Text | Themes | ABAR Lens for Lessons and Discussions | Possible Paired Texts | Standards |
|---|---|---|---|---|
| *The Adventures of Tom Sawyer* by Mark Twain | Childhood and innocence or coming of age | ▪ How does the American childhood experience differ depending on the racial identity of the child?<br>▪ Analyze the historical context, author's perspective, and racial and gender biases revealed through characters like Injun Joe and Becky Sawyer. | ▪ Excerpts from *Narrative of the Life of Frederick Douglass* and *All American Boys* by Jason Reynolds | CCSS.ELA-LITERACY.RL.6.9 Compare and contrast texts in different forms or genres (e.g., stories and poems; historical novels and fantasy stories) in terms of their approaches to similar themes and topics. |
| *Island of the Blue Dolphins* by Scott O'Dell | Environmentalism | ▪ Why do "own voices" texts (texts that are written by authors who share the same identity or history as their subjects) matter?<br>▪ While the book sheds light on animal cruelty, in what ways are Indigenous people stereotyped? | ▪ *Island of the Blue Dolphins: The Complete Reader's Edition* edited by Sara L. Schwebel<br>▪ *Indian No More* by Charlene Willing McManis, Traci Sorell<br>▪ *Stone River Crossing* by Tim Tingle | CCSS.ELA-LITERACY.RL.4.6 Compare and contrast the point of view from which different stories are narrated, including the difference between first- and third-person narrations. |

*(continues)*

FIGURE 2–3 Teaching Mandated Texts Through an ABAR Lens *(continued)*

| Mandated Text | Themes | ABAR Lens for Lessons and Discussions | Possible Paired Texts | Standards |
|---|---|---|---|---|
| **Books by Dr. Seuss (this often comes up during Read Across America Day)** | Stereotyping | ■ Should authors who have acted or spoken in discriminatory ways be celebrated? | ■ Dr. Seuss' original political cartoons<br>■ Articles on Roald Dahl's antisemitism | **CCSS.ELA-LITERACY.RH.6-8.6** Identify aspects of a text that reveal an author's point of view or purpose (e.g., loaded language, inclusion or avoidance of particular facts). |
| ***To Kill a Mockingbird* by Harper Lee** | Justice, racism, saviorism | ■ How is whiteness constructed in this text?<br>■ Whose perspective is represented in this book?<br>■ How and where does saviorism show up in the text? | ■ *Just Mercy* by Bryan Stevenson<br>■ *Stamped: A Remix* by Jason Reynolds and Ibram X. Kendi<br>■ *I Know Why the Caged Bird Sings* by Maya Angelou<br>■ Excerpts from *White Trash: The 400-Year Untold History of Class in America* by Nancy Isenberg | **CCSS.ELA-LITERACY.RI.6.7** Integrate information presented in different media or formats as well as in words to develop a coherent understanding of a topic or issue. |

## { KEEP IN MIND }

"I was one of two white educators in my school. We were putting together information on alternatives to Dr. Seuss for Read Across America. We wanted to explain to everyone why we weren't celebrating Dr. Seuss, and we shared information from The Conscious Kid that included a photo comparing someone in black face to *The Cat in the Hat*. We didn't think about or realize the trauma connected to that for Black teachers in the community. So that was a big mess-up. A lot of our African American educators told us that was not OK. That made me realize that I really need to make sure I'm stepping back and checking where other people are coming from, think about other people's perspectives, and even if I have good intentions, how it might impact people. Even with the best of intentions, this was still not OK."

—SKYE TOOLEY (THEY/THEM)

# Taking Action in the Classroom: Build Trust

Building a culture of trust and respect in the classroom is imperative if we want students to be open, honest, and communicative. Teachers must take the time to understand their students—who they are, and where they're coming from.

## Stay Connected by Being Vulnerable

Brené Brown reminds us, "Staying vulnerable is a risk we have to take if we want to experience connection." If I'm asking my students to share themselves and be vulnerable with me and their peers in the classroom, it's important that I lead by example. I'll often open the school year by sharing my own identity during community-building activities, and discussing my experience as a student. I tell my students about a math teacher who made me cry in class and convinced me I was a terrible math student. I tell them that my grades in middle and high school were far from perfect, and that grades are only one measurement of understanding and academic success. I'm also honest with them when I've experienced a loss in my life, or sometimes when I'm having an off day. One of the most powerful classroom conversations I had was when I told students that I would be taking a mental health day. It allowed a few students to feel comfortable talking about their own emotions and experiences with therapy. We cannot expect or demand our students to share who they are if we are not willing to do the same.

## } KEEP IN MIND {

"White teachers have to start by examining themselves. Don't start the conversation by asking students to talk about their identities. You have to model that you're able to talk about your identity, too. The reality is that over 80 percent of teachers are white, cisgender, women, and if that's you and you can't talk about it, you're putting more of a burden on your students."

—CODY MILLER (HE/HIM)

## Get a Sense of How Students Feel with a Quick Check-In

Take a look at your teaching blocks and think about where you have some flexibility. These don't have to be huge chunks of time. It might be a ten- or fifteen-minute window at the beginning or end of the day (during arrival or dismissal) to read aloud, or have students write or talk about a certain topic. Those few minutes add up and can help grow and support an ABAR classroom culture.

On days when we had early dismissal, unit tests, or standardized assessments, I often looked at my week's to-do list and worried about fitting in everything we had to cover. No matter how hectic the week was, there were always three short times of the day that were consistently available: morning meeting, our post-lunch read-aloud, and closing circle. My school's morning arrival and afternoon dismissal windows spanned fifteen minutes each. These were opportune times for students to start thinking about a new topic, or to reflect on a topic we had previously discussed. When they arrived every day, there would be a check-in question on the board, like the one in Figure 2–4. They were free to write as little or as much as they liked, but all students had to show me their journal response, like the one in Figure 2–5. It was a quick and easy way to check in with them individually and get a sense of how they were feeling that day.

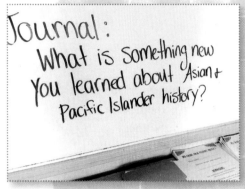

FIGURE 2-4 Morning Journal Check-In Question

Something new I learned about Asian Pacific Islanders was that Hawaii was its own country but it was overcome by the US. The Hawaiian king died so the queen took his place. The queen had to make a treaty with the US to protect her people.

FIGURE 2-5 Student Response to Morning Journal Check-In Question

## Explore Stereotypes

Present students with correct terminology and help them understand the meaning of the word by making connections to prior knowledge and asking questions. In my second-grade class, starting with language was important, especially since a handful of my students were emerging bilinguals. I presented them with the term *stereotype*. To help them understand the meaning of the word, I asked, "How are teachers often shown in movies or TV shows?" My students were highly amused and enjoyed listing descriptions like "Teachers are strict," "They wag their fingers at you and tell you to be quiet," and "They're old and mean and look like someone's grandma." We created a chart like the one in Figure 2–6. Afterward, I asked my class if their

FIGURE 2-6 Teacher Stereotypes chart

### Stereotypes About Teachers

- All teachers are old.
- All teachers are mean.
- All teachers are strict.
- All teachers are bossy and like bossing kids around.
- All teachers are women.
- All teachers wag their finger at kids.
- All teachers act like they don't like students.
- All teachers like giving homework and pop quizzes.

preschool, kindergarten, or first-grade teachers fit these descriptions. Nearly every student disagreed. From this discussion, we built our understanding of stereotypes as a widely held but overly simple idea of a person or group. Stereotypes can sometimes seem complimentary (one student added, "People who wear glasses are smart!") but don't leave room for individual experiences or identities. They also can be used as a tool for gatekeeping. We ended this initial lesson by sharing perceived stereotypes of children. My students were hyperaware of how adults often unfairly perceived them to be loud, unruly, unintelligent, and dirty.

Since Halloween was approaching and my students were swapping ideas about their favorite costumes and characters, this felt like an opportune moment to apply our understanding of stereotypes to a real-world situation. We collected toy and costume catalogues and distributed them to groups of students. Their instructions were simple: Cut and sort the toys and costumes based on gender stereotypes. (In recent years, I've added more inclusive language around gender to this activity, but students are still able to recognize the amount of toy and clothing marketing directed toward children that exists along a gender binary.) The students and I observed their sorting. We looked for patterns, generated questions, debated the potential impact on children who receive these gendered messages, and created a chart like the one in Figure 2–7. One student shared that she wanted to be the Karate Kid for Halloween, but when her family went shopping for a costume, the outfit in the "Girls" section came in only one color: bright pink. When she ventured into the "Boys" aisle, her brother teased her for wearing a "boy costume."

FIGURE 2–7 Halloween Costumes chart

Over the next few days, my students began volunteering more examples of gender stereotypes they noticed outside of school. One boy talked about being teased for being "girly" because he colored his nails with a marker. A girl vented about a movie she had watched where the main female character kept making irresponsible choices and repeatedly needed to be saved by a boy. Our upcoming reading unit focused on fairy and folk tales, during which the kids reveled in pointing out problematic gender roles. We talked about how the main female character in most fairy tales did not have any female friends, and relationships between female characters were strained due to jealousy over physical appearance or romantic interests. We also discussed how the male characters were presented as hypermasculine, athletic, and unemotional, which led to a deeply personal community circle where the boys in class shared their feelings about the pressure to adhere to similar expectations from peers or family members. We made a chart about expectations for men, like the one in Figure 2–8. Throughout this unit, we simultaneously hit ELA standards about plot, cause and effect, and character analysis, all while developing a critical lens for gender stereotyping.

Our work around gender also helped enhance our persuasive writing unit and mathematics application. My students were able to apply the skills from the curriculum—stating their opinions, using evidence, and providing suggestions—but directed their writing to companies that manufactured and sold toys and kids' clothing. We also pulled price

FIGURE 2–8 Expectations for Men chart

| Stereotypes and Expectations of Men and Boys | |
|---|---|
| **Cause** | **Effect** |
| Boys are supposed to play sports. | Some boys feel pressured to play sports even when they don't want to. |
| Boys are supposed to be serious and strong. | You can be teased and called "weak." |
| Boys are supposed to be tough. | |
| Boys are supposed to like girls. | People act shocked if a boy doesn't like girls.<br>■ Some boys are gay. |
| Boys can't like rainbows or unicorns or wear pink or purple. | Makes you feel like you have to change what you like or else people might not hang out with you. |
| Boys are supposed to "man up." | Boys are afraid of being called girly.<br>■ It's not OK to use being a girl as a put-down.<br>■ Makes you feel not good enough. |

comparisons for the same products marketed toward men and toward women and calculated how much more women were expected to pay for items such as bike helmets, deodorant, and haircuts of similar length. (We had a separate lesson on the "pink tax" and gender pay disparities.)

The unit culminated with a discussion about what is being done in the world to dispel gender stereotypes. We identified steps we could take in our own lives. My students generated ideas about how to respond on the playground if someone made a stereotypical remark. We talked about ways that we pushed back against gender norms. We also read books that countered gender stereotypes, and analyzed commercials and marketing campaigns that strived to break away from stereotypes in favor of inclusion. Ultimately we met the goal to develop students' social consciousness while still making sure we handled our academic business.

# Creating a Sustainable Practice: Reflect on Lessons

Even when teachers have evidence that students are walking away from class with a more developed critical lens, lesson reflection is a necessary step that is often overlooked or forgotten in the daily classroom bustle. I have now taught the unit on gender stereotyping for many years, and each year it looks a little different. Some of the changes are based on my own learning and unlearning, such as making sure I was being inclusive of nonbinary and trans students and wasn't reinforcing the gender binary. Other changes took place simply because each year I have a new class of students with different backgrounds, needs, and questions. Veteran educators can risk falling into the comfortable routine of repeating the same lessons and using the same materials every year, but teachers must pay attention to how language and ABAR ideas are evolving in our society. This does not mean that lessons have to be completely rewritten every year, but we do need to audit them to see what needs to be updated based on current events and the learners in our classroom.

## How Do I Know If It's Working?

Return to your ABAR curriculum and standards planner from Figure 2–2 and ask yourself how things went and what changes you need to make. Take a look at my reflections for the first two subjects—ELA and writing—in Figure 2–9. You'll find a blank template for this form in the online resources.

### ABAR Curriculum and Standards Planner and Reflection

OR 2–1

| Subject | What do I *have* to do in order to do what I *want* to do? | How can I tackle this through an ABAR lens? | What/where can I supplement/substitute? | How did this go? What changes do I need to make? |
|---|---|---|---|---|
| English Language Arts | I have to teach a unit on fairy tales that uses multiple versions of *Cinderella*. | ▪ I can teach about gender norms and gendered language.<br>▪ I can lead discussions about how fairy tales can impact our ideas of gender expectations. | ▪ I can add to this unit by comparing and contrasting other fairy and folk tales that counter stereotypes of male saviorism and female competition. | ▪ Overall, the lessons went well, but I found that many students had a difficult time moving away from gender-binary language. In the future I need to be more explicit about identities along the gender spectrum. |
| Writing | I have to teach my students lessons on grammar and sentence structure. | ▪ I can take time to learn about my students' backgrounds and make connections to their home languages.<br>▪ I can commit to never shaming my students for mispronouncing words.<br>▪ I can be aware of biases I may have toward students who are emerging bilinguals or who speak with an accent. | ▪ I can teach about how letter-sound correspondence differs across languages.<br>▪ I can teach about AAVE (African American Vernacular English) as its own language.<br>▪ I can teach my students about code switching and how different contexts sometimes require different types of writing. | ▪ The emerging bilingual students were very excited to teach their classmates words in their home languages. Maybe next time we can also learn about where ideas of "standard English" come from, and how standardization automatically leaves some people out. |

FIGURE 2–9 Sample ABAR Curriculum and Standards Planner and Reflection

## Check on Classroom Culture

Even though feedback is a large part of a teacher's practice, receiving feedback about our own teaching can be hard to hear. Most educators choose this career path because of a deep-seated passion, and when our identities are tied too closely to our work, feedback feels personal. I like to view feedback as a gift, and my friend and colleague shea martin (they/them) taught me the importance of viewing accountability as an act of love. If I love my students, it's my responsibility to ask for their feedback, reflect on it, and adapt my practice.

About every other month, I ask my students to evaluate our classroom culture and my teaching by filling out a form like the one in Figure 2–10. I joke with my classes that while the principal is my employer, I actually work for my students. I enjoy recording their input in graphs and charts so we can discuss the patterns we see as a class and share honestly about our experiences. Figure 2–11 shows their responses to the

> I feel comfortable asking Ms. Kleinrock for help or expressing questions when I'm confused
>
> ○ Strongly disagree
>
> ○ Disagree
>
> ○ Neutral
>
> ○ Agree
>
> ○ Strongly agree
>
> What parts of English class are you enjoying? What is going well?
>
> Short answer text
>
> Any suggestions on how to improve English class?
>
> Long answer text

FIGURE 2–10 Class Evaluation

> Any suggestions on how to improve English class?
> 51 responses
>
> no I like it the way it is
>
> I guess more check-ins, because sometimes we might not have the clearest view on our work and could have the teacher give an opinion or feedback
>
> Having more time to work on our own personal narrative.
>
> I would like to have more self paced work personally.
>
> reading and narrative
>
> No it really good
>
> I don't really have anything right at this moment, but If there's anything i would eventually reach out to you
>
> no i like how it is
>
> I think it would be better if we had just a little more time to do the classwork for English class

FIGURE 2–11 Student Evaluation Sample Responses

final question in the evaluation. Figure 2–12 is a graph of their responses to a follow-up statement based on a pattern I noticed in their responses.

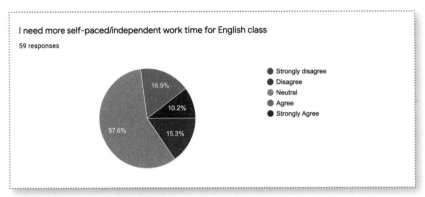

**I need more self-paced/independent work time for English class**
59 responses

- Strongly disagree
- Disagree
- Neutral
- Agree
- Strongly Agree

16.9%
10.2%
57.6%
15.3%

FIGURE 2–12 Evaluation Question Response Breakdown

## Don't Reinvent the Wheel

ABAR practices are new initiatives for many teachers and schools, but there are resources out there from organizations and educators who have written about and shared their practices. For example, educators Tricia Ebarvia (she/her), Lorena Germán (she/her), Dr. Kimberly Parker (she/her), and Julia Torres (she/her) built #DisruptTexts "to challenge the traditional canon in order to create a more inclusive, representative, and equitable language arts curriculum." Their website and social media community provide a space for educators to listen, learn, and share successful practices. Additionally, founders of #THEBOOKCHAT Scott Bayer (he/him) and Joel Garza (he/him) created a resource to help teachers identify ways to create more culturally inclusive curricula. As most teachers are not able to completely abandon their curriculum or required texts (however problematic they may be), Bayer and Garza suggested pairing or supplementing traditional texts with more recent and inclusive titles. For example, Harper Lee's *To Kill a Mockingbird*, which centers a white savior narrative, might be paired with Bryan Stevenson's *Just Mercy*, which explores his experience as a Black lawyer fighting against systemic racism in the criminal justice system.

{3}

# How Can I Hold Space for Difficult Conversations in My Class?

**DURING THE OPENING OF MY TED TALK,** "How to Teach Kids to Talk About Taboo Topics," I describe an uncomfortable situation that occurred in my fourth-grade classroom (Kleinrock 2019). During an introductory conversation about the social construction of race, my students were filling in a chart with things they already knew about race as well as questions they had on the subject. One student posed the question, "Why are people racist?" Another girl whom I called "Abby" raised her hand and volunteered, "Maybe white people don't like Black people because they think their skin is the color of poop."

Right on cue, half of the class burst out laughing, and the other half admonished her and scolded, "You can't say that!" This all played out within less than a minute, during which I had to process the remark and the students' reactions, plus determine how I would respond. After a few seconds, I made the decision to call my class to the carpet to unpack Abby's comment. (I want to note that Abby is a non-Black person of color and remind educators that ABAR work is essential for *all* students because anti-Blackness is a universal issue.) I explained that her hypothesis about racial bias is a belief that has been shared by many people throughout history, and that one reason racial discrimination exists is because having darker skin is seen as less attractive than light skin. Therefore, the reason why we learn about these ideas and have these conversations is to understand why these comments are harmful, and to educate ourselves to know better and do better.

There isn't one correct way to handle situations when a student makes a biased remark, and there are parts of how I responded that I would change if the same situation arose in the future. After the talk was released, one viewer commented that I shouldn't allow ignorance in my classroom, but I disagree. If there was no ignorance in my classroom, there would be no students. A huge challenge of antibias and antiracist work begins when people start to unpack what biases or racist beliefs they hold. Sometimes these get put on display. We have to be able to recognize and name problems if we ever hope to find solutions. Nonetheless I do believe that ignorance should never go unaddressed, especially when it is publicly displayed, as in Abby's case.

While Abby was certainly embarrassed, I monitored her interactions with other students. She didn't seem to be ostracized by peers. During a break, I quickly checked in with other students of color in the class and alerted Abby's family about her comment and the discussion that followed. Even though this crisis was averted, it's my belief that toxic environments are created when adults witness biased actions and words from children and fail to address them. Sweeping comments under the rug or harshly reprimanding students who don't understand the gravity of their words contribute to an environment of mistrust. Kids can tell when the adults in their lives center their own comfort over the protection of children. When our children make these kinds of statements in public, most parents and caregivers are mortified. Adults will break into fight-or-flight mode, responding harshly "Don't be rude!" or silently ushering their child away and muttering apologies. But when a student makes a racially charged comment (whether intentional or unintentional) in class, it is our job as educators to address it.

Quite often this is easier said than done. When our relatives make problematic remarks during the holidays, most of us still go wide-eyed and exchange silent, horrified looks but fail to speak up. With our families and friends, we often think of silence as a way of "keeping the peace," yet what this really means is that we're avoiding a situation where people may feel uncomfortable. While this approach may temporarily save your holiday gathering, this does not work in a classroom environment. Your number one job is to center your students, not your own feelings. (However, for teachers who hold marginalized identities, self-care practices are necessary, which may include taking time to process a comment made by a peer or a student that triggers a prior trauma before responding.)

# Setting Yourself Up for Success: Intentionally Cultivate Your Classroom Culture

While we cannot predict the words that come out of our students' mouths, no one wants to be caught like a deer in the headlights when someone makes an offensive remark in class. We want to be fluent in ABAR language, comprehend how words fit within specific contexts, and not feel panicked grasping for the right thing to say in moments of high emotion.

When someone says something offensive, how often do we find ourselves agonizing about what we wish we had said? In order to avoid these retrospective fantasies, it's important to consider how you want to approach these situations with students. Just as when we exercise consistently to train and strengthen our muscles, the only way to become stronger and more confident in responding to problematic remarks is to engage in conversation.

## Be Aware of Your Own Reactions and Boundaries

While comments like Abby's might not intend to harm, students must learn the importance of owning their impact. Sometimes students will push boundaries to see what kinds of remarks they can get away with, claim they're "just kidding," or that they're "exercising their first amendment rights" if adults or peers push back. Certain comments made by students may trigger their classmates and teachers, and as challenging as it may be, teachers are expected to model measured responses. This does not mean you should allow students to say harmful things to you, but rather how can you hold a firm boundary while also holding the student accountable?

When someone makes a harmful remark in front of us, our instincts typically tell us to respond combatively, avoid and change the subject, or lose our train of thought (fight, flight, or freeze). Use Figure 3–1 to reflect on your common instincts and be aware of how you tend to respond. We can prepare responses to meet our own needs and create teachable moments.

FIGURE 3-1 Fight Flight Freeze

| If you tend to . . . | |
| --- | --- |
| Fight | "Your comment does not reflect the values of our classroom community. Can you explain why you made that choice?" |
| Flight | "I'm having a reaction to what you just said and need a few minutes to collect my thoughts before we talk." |
| Freeze | "What did you mean by that comment?" |

## Practice Calling In

One effective response is to "call someone in," meaning we invite someone into a conversation in order to both educate and hold the person accountable for their words or actions. It's different from a *callout*, which can be used to interrupt a harmful comment or behavior. Calling someone in shows the other person that what they said was unacceptable. While I believe there is a time and a place for each strategy, when working with students I try to use these instances as teachable moments. Author and activist Loretta J. Ross has written extensively about calling others in, rather than calling them out. In an article for *Learning for Justice*, Ross explains:

Calling in is not for everyone or every circumstance. It's not fair, for example, to insist that people hurt by cruel or careless language or actions be responsible for the personal growth of those who have injured them; calling in should not demand involuntary emotional labor.

Calling in is also not a useful response to those who intentionally violate standards of civil conversation. When powerful people use bigotry, fear and lies to attack others, calling out can be a valuable tool, either for the individuals they seek to oppress or for bystanders who choose to interrupt the encounter. When people knowingly use stereotypes or dehumanizing metaphors to describe human beings, their actions victimize targets and potentially set them up for violence. Calling out may be the best response to those who refuse to accept responsibility for the harm they encourage or who pretend they are only innocently using their right to free speech. (2019, 19)

A good place to start is to consider how you would want to be called in if you made a problematic remark in front of others. The goal is not to shame anyone, but to create a learning opportunity for the student in question as well as for your class community. Try using the chart in Figure 3–2 to practice these conversations.

At the end of the day, students need spaces where they can be vulnerable and brave in order to learn. Teachers are also learners. They need to draw on their vulnerability and courage in order to best support their students. Throughout my years in the classroom, I have heard kids of all backgrounds make comments about people's races, cultures, accents, food, religious clothing, abilities—you name it. Many of their remarks stem from ignorance, and I expect this from them because they're children. Shaming kids for their ignorance is unproductive. All it does is teach them to fear being wrong or asking questions. Shaming encourages them to disengage. Oftentimes, the alternative simply looks like telling your students: "That's a good question. I actually don't know the answer. Let's figure it out together."

**FIGURE 3-2** Possible Call-In Conversations

| Comment | Knee-Jerk Reaction | Interrupting Strategy | Call-In Conversation |
|---|---|---|---|
| "That's so gay." | "Never say that. That is mean, cruel, and beyond disrespectful." | "That language makes me uncomfortable. I'm wondering if you know the impact of your words when you say, 'That's so gay.' Can you explain why you said that?" | "I understand that some people use the phrase 'That's so gay' when they really mean something is dull or boring. However, I want you to understand that it's very hurtful to people who identify as LGBTQ+ and can make them feel hurt and unwelcome. How do you think it might make a queer person feel if they heard you say that? Is there another phrase you can use instead?" |
| "Kelly can't play with us because her skin is Black. She's dirty." | "That's a rude thing to say and point out. It doesn't matter what skin color she has!" | "Different people have different color skin, and it's OK to notice these differences because our skin colors are beautiful. However, it's not OK to make people feel bad or exclude them because of their skin color." | "I understand that when someone looks different, we often feel curious. Did you know that our skin color comes from a few different sources, like the color of our ancestors' skin, and something called *melanin*? Melanin is something in our skin that causes some people to tan or get darker when they're in the sun. People with dark skin like Kelly most likely came from places that had a lot of strong sunlight. In our communities, there have been a lot of people who said that dark skin wasn't as good as light skin, and they treated Black and Brown people badly because of this difference. Do you think it's fair to treat people poorly because of what they look like?" |

*(continues)*

FIGURE 3–2 Possible Call-In Conversations *(continued)*

| Comment | Knee-Jerk Reaction | Interrupting Strategy | Call-In Conversation |
|---|---|---|---|
| "My parents said that Muslims are terrorists." | "Why would you say something so unkind? If you can't say something nice, don't say anything at all." | "I'm curious why you chose to repeat that opinion. Do you personally know any people who are Muslim? I'm wondering if you've thought about how repeating that statement might make your Muslim classmates feel, or your classmates who have Muslim family members or friends." | "In our classroom we try to avoid stereotyping. A stereotype is a widely oversimplified statement about a particular group of people. While your parents may have those views, and there are often negative stereotypes of Muslim people on TV and in the media, it's unfair and inaccurate to say that an entire group of people are terrorists. Comments like these sometimes result in Muslim people being targeted because of their beliefs and appearance, and it's important to understand and respect differences rather than labeling others in negative ways." |
| "All white people are bad because white people owned slaves." | "That's a terrible thing to say. You don't need to make white people feel guilty for things that happened years ago." | "I understand why some people might feel this way, but I think we also need to address why it's problematic to speak in generalizations and make statements and claims about entire groups of people." | "First of all, let's acknowledge that white people who enslaved Black people did terrible things. There has been a long history of racist beliefs and laws in the United States that have been upheld by white people, and many white people continue to benefit from these beliefs and laws to this day. I don't think it's fair to state that all white people are bad for things their ancestors did. I do think it's important to hold white people accountable because they continue to benefit from racism, or if they aren't doing anything to put a stop to racism in their community." |

# Taking Action in the Classroom: Learn How Students Feel Talking About Certain Topics

Diving into topics around ABAR requires intentional planning. The first time I explicitly tackled race in the classroom with my fourth graders, I was incredibly anxious because I didn't know how my students would engage in the conversations. We had learned about the history of enslavement and talked about different forms of oppression and injustice. But we had never explicitly talked about race as a social construct or analyzed racist structures and biases. I realized that before we began, I needed to get on the same page as my students and learn how they felt about the subject matter.

## ❴ KEEP IN MIND ❵

"Teachers probably have to work on getting over their fear of mistakes because we're all trying this great social experiment called social justice. And so, nine out of 10 things we try are going to be errors. And it's like riding a bike; you get back up and you ride it again. So, we're going to have to get over our fear of falling and our fear of errors so that we can be brave together. There are lots of resources for educators who want to learn how to have these difficult dialogues, but the first step is overcoming our fear of the conversation in the first place."

—LORETTA ROSS

## Establish Group Ethos or Agreements

If you've ever participated in an ABAR or diversity-related workshop, the facilitator most likely opened with group norming, or agreements. I tend to avoid the term *norms*, as this language often reflects the values of the dominant group or culture. With young people and adults, I prefer to use *community ethos*, which focuses on characteristics and values that we take with us from space to space (not just within the workshop or classroom setting), or *community agreements* if they are truly co-constructed by the entire group. A teacher should not write a list of rules to present to their students and call them agreements. By intentionally discussing communication styles and delivery, students can take ownership of this space and consider how they can set themselves up to be heard by their peers.

In Figure 3–3, you can observe the agreements created by Abby and her classmates. Writing agreements does not mean you will be free of

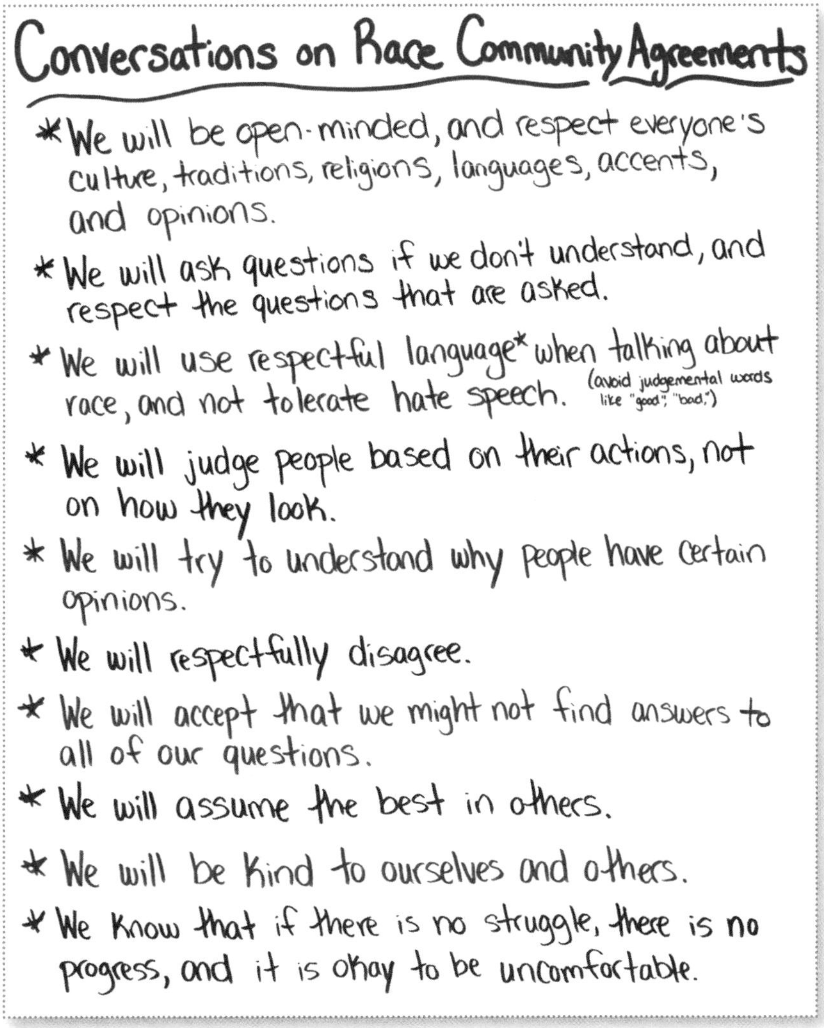

# Conversations on Race Community Agreements

* We will be open-minded, and respect everyone's culture, traditions, religions, languages, accents, and opinions.
* We will ask questions if we don't understand, and respect the questions that are asked.
* We will use respectful language* when talking about race, and not tolerate hate speech. (avoid judgemental words like "good", "bad".)
* We will judge people based on their actions, not on how they look.
* We will try to understand why people have certain opinions.
* We will respectfully disagree.
* We will accept that we might not find answers to all of our questions.
* We will assume the best in others.
* We will be kind to ourselves and others.
* We know that if there is no struggle, there is no progress, and it is okay to be uncomfortable.

FIGURE 3-3 Fourth-Grade Group Agreements

conflict, but they provide important reminders that you can reference if the conversation seems to be moving in an unproductive or harmful direction.

Based on Marshall Rosenberg's (2003) writing on nonviolent communication, I structure this dialogue by identifying our needs as a community and what we can agree to do in order to fulfill these needs. For example, in conversations about social identities and differences, the need for trust and respect is crucial. If we need to build trust with one another and interact respectfully, what concrete steps can we commit to that will meet these needs? In Figures 3–4a–c, you can see examples of how I structured this activity with my sixth-grade students during our first week of school.

## THE FOUNDATION OF ALL RELATIONSHIPS: [A]

### TRUST        RESPECT

In breakout rooms, share your definitions of what these two words mean to you.

- What does it mean to show trust and respect?
- What does it mean to receive trust and respect?
- What does it look like/sound like?
- How does it feel?

## WHAT ARE OUR NEEDS AS LEARNERS? [B]

| Our words and actions show what our needs might be, and if they are/aren't being met. | Sample Needs: | Group Learning: |
|---|---|---|
| | • The need to trust and be trusted.<br>• The need for respect.<br>• The need to feel safe.<br>• The need to communicate.<br>• The need to feel seen and valued as a person. | • How can we support each other and ourselves to meet these needs? |

## EXAMPLE: THE NEED FOR SAFETY AND TRUST. [C]

We can fulfill this need by:
- Physical safety:
  » Keeping our hands, feet, and objects to ourselves.
  » Wearing masks and washing our hands.
- Emotional safety/trust:
  » Expecting and respecting when people make mistakes.
  » Using inclusive language that honors who people are (ex: using people's correct pronouns).

FIGURE 3–4A–C Sixth-Grade Community Ethos

## Learn from Questionnaires

There are many ways to distribute questionnaires on paper or through
a digital form. You can use a bar graph with sticky notes like the one in
Figure 3–7, a paper questionnaire as shown in Figure 3–5, or an online
form as seen in Figures 3–6a–b. In these questionnaires, I simply ask
my students to rate their comfort level talking about race and racism
on a scale from one to five (one meaning very uncomfortable, and
five meaning very comfortable), and leave a space for them to explain their self-assessment if they choose. After the questionnaires
are returned, I can create a large bar graph showing the distribution
of every student's ranking (tools such as Google Forms will do this
for you automatically). Together you and your students can observe
trends and, anonymously, some individual responses if students grant

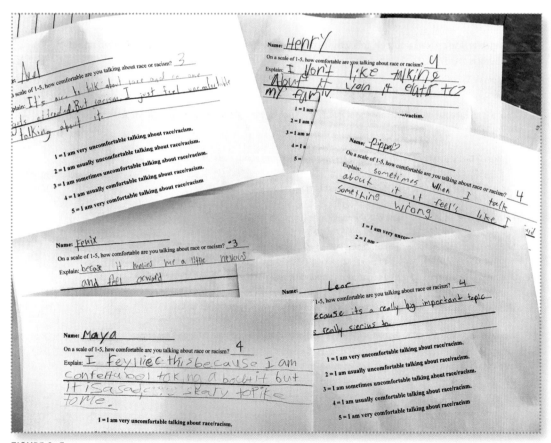

FIGURE 3–5 Paper Questionnaires About Race

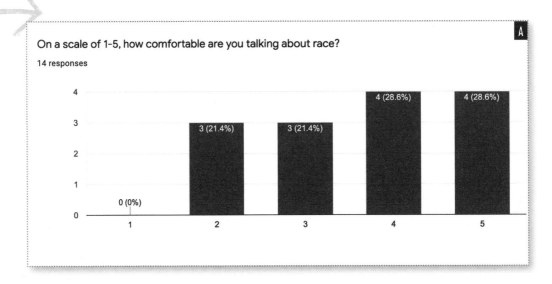

On a scale of 1-5, how comfortable are you talking about race?

14 responses

A

Explain why you ranked yourself this way. (Ex: If you gave yourself a 4 comfort level talking about race, why is this?)

14 responses

B

I put a 2 on race because i can talk about it but i don't like to. I put a 3 on politics because im comfortable on it. like to talk abo

I ranked 2 because I dont really like racis people and studying about racisim

Because i want to learn it and i dont have a problrm

i still have friends that are black but are really nice (i am not racist)

because i don't seem to get embarrassed talking about race like some others

The reason I gave my self a 5 because I talk about race and politics with family and friends

My dads very political and he always is talking politics with me so i got used to it.

I enjoy talking about politics but with race it is kind of sensitive since I am African - American

its ok becuase people talk about it every day so im use to it

FIGURE 3-6A-B Digital Questionnaires About Race

you permission. If students are comfortable with their thoughts being shared, it can be a validating experience for those who feel hesitant to talk about these subjects. As I read a few opinions in one of my classes, many students expressed relief and a shared connection when a few classmates shared such sentiments as "I want to talk about race, but I'm so scared of saying something racist!" or "Sometimes when I talk about it, it feels like I said something wrong." Once students recognize that many of their classmates have the same worries and concerns, their initial feelings of discomfort transform into more courage to question and have dialogue.

If you don't want to use an individual online or paper survey, consider a chart questionnaire conducted as a gallery walk. A chart questionnaire offers flexibility because you can get immediate responses to a question or questions. Teachers can write different questions at the top of the chart papers and ask students to either answer directly on the

FIGURE 3–7 Chart Questionnaires About Race

chart or write their answers on a sticky note and place it on the chart. Figure 3–7 shows students placing their responses to questions on two charts: "Does race matter? Is it important?" and "Does your race matter to you? Why or why not?" Notice how the students on the left are reading the responses while the student on the right is placing a sticky note onto the chart.

## Open Students' Minds to Other Perspectives but Interrupt When Necessary

Nearly every educator I've worked with has their own version of my Abby story. Music teacher Czarina Francisco Jimenez (she/siya) recalled a student asking an Asian classmate, "Don't you eat dog?" ESL teacher Melissa Garcia (she/her) shared a time when a student had assumed she was married to a man, and when she explained that her partner is a woman, the student responded, "That's weird!" Other teachers have shared stories of students making homophobic and ableist remarks such as "That's so gay" or "Are you deaf or something?" and telling Latinx students that they're going to be deported. What does it sound like to interrupt these comments in a way that allows them to become teachable moments for students?

Recently, my students decided they wanted to investigate the cause and possible solutions for the Los Angeles housing crisis that has resulted in thousands of people experiencing homelessness. In the neighborhood around our school, there were multiple encampments of people experiencing homelessness, and it was a common topic in the parent Facebook group to worry and bicker over the location of the school, the cleanliness of the neighborhood, and the safety of the students. This deficit-based language did not go unnoticed by my students.

When we began reading articles about the housing crisis and rising numbers of people who were without housing in California, a few comments came up when we began to chart questions about the issue:

TEACHER: "What do we think we know about the housing crisis and people in our community experiencing homelessness?"

WYATT: "My dad says homeless people don't have jobs because they're lazy."

CHARLIE: "That's a really mean thing to say!"

WYATT: "What? It's true. If they weren't lazy, they'd get jobs."

TEACHER: "Let's take a minute to talk about this, because I have a feeling that a lot of people in our community probably have the same opinion. Wyatt, you mentioned that your dad has this opinion, but do you think this is true?"

WYATT: "Yeah. I don't know. Why don't they just get jobs?"

TEACHER: "I can see how from an outside perspective it might seem really easy for someone to get a job. We see people with different jobs all the time. But what kinds of reasons might make it hard for someone to get a job?"

EMMA: "Like if they're sick. Or they live in a car."

TEACHER: "Being sick would absolutely make it hard for someone to get a job. I know that when I feel sick, it's really hard to come to school. I'm lucky because our school gives teachers sick days, so we don't get in trouble for staying home if we have a cold. But what if a person has the type of sickness where it takes them a very long time to feel better?"

WYATT: "I guess so. They could still do some work though."

TEACHER: "That's true, there are lots of different types of work. But we also have to recognize that just because someone has a job and makes money doesn't mean they can afford to live in a place like Los Angeles. What if a person has a job that pays them ten dollars an hour, but the job only needs them to work twenty hours a week? Two hundred dollars a week might seem like a lot of money, but most apartments in this city cost over one thousand dollars a month. So a person might have a job, make some money, but not have enough to afford a home."

WYATT: "So they have to live in their car?"

TEACHER: "Sometimes. People who live in cars are still experiencing homelessness."

WYATT: "Oh. I didn't know that. But I still think they should try to work."

Having an epiphany in class is incredibly rare. I did not expect to change Wyatt's mind, but rather to open him up to the possibility of another perspective. During this conversation, the other students were agitated and attempted to interject with angry remarks to disprove his theory, and when this occurred Wyatt would get defensive. While this conversation took time and centered on his comment, it was an important opportunity to model for the other students how questioning and connecting with someone who holds a different opinion can be a powerful tool for engaging respectfully across differences.

On other occasions, a discussion isn't an appropriate strategy, especially if a student has just uttered a comment that can be deemed offensive to another person's identity or that minimizes the humanity of a person or group. When it comes to the safety and inclusion of differences in your classroom, it is the teacher's responsibility to draw boundaries and set expectations of acceptable behavior and language. Hate speech isn't something that is up for debate. It's nonnegotiable.

Outward biases and stereotypes need to be addressed immediately before they're absorbed and perpetuated by other students. Nearly every year when my class learns about LGBTQ+ identities and diverse family structures, a student makes a comment that needs to be interrupted:

TEACHER: "Who can give some examples of different types of families? For example, I'm adopted, and I don't look like my mom or dad. There are certainly other families with adopted children in the world, but most families don't look like mine."

CHRISTIAN: "Some kids live with their aunt or grandma."

JACKIE: "My parents are divorced. I live with my mom on school days and I live with my dad and my stepmom on the weekend."

MICHAEL: "Some families have two moms or two dads."

NATALIE: "Two dads? That's gross and so weird."

TEACHER: "I'm actually going to stop you there. In our community, there are lots of different types of families. Using words like *gross* and *weird* to describe people is disrespectful and we don't use language like that to talk about differences. However, it's OK to ask questions and be curious about people who are different or new to you."

Natalie's comment came quickly and could have easily derailed the entire lesson on families. In these moments, interrupting is necessary because allowing negative remarks about differences will have a lasting impact on your classroom culture. The teacher's response is immediate and firm, but most importantly, the closing remark offers an alternative action to the student in order for the response to end on a proactive rather than punitive note.

A few years ago, I attended a talk led by Dr. Beverly Daniel Tatum, author of the acclaimed *Why Are All the Black Kids Sitting Together in the Cafeteria?* (2017). She suggested that a simple and effective way to respond to biased remarks is to establish a connection and present an alternative way of thinking: "You know, I used to think that too. But then I learned _____, and now I think _____."

Additionally, Ross (2019) gives a few examples of sentence frames that educators can familiarize themselves with and use in these moments:

>> "I need to stop you there because something you just said is not accurate."

>> "I'm having a reaction to that comment. Let's go back for a minute."

>> "Do you think you would say that if someone from that group was with us in the room?"

>> "There's some history behind that expression you just used that you might not know about."

>> "In this class, we hold each other accountable. So we need to talk about why that joke isn't funny." (19)

## } KEEP IN MIND {

"Teachers have an obligation to set boundaries. Because their highest obligation is to create a safe learning environment . . . The best learning cannot take place in an atmosphere of insults, punishments, and people not taking responsibility for the consequences of what they say. Sometimes, when people demand free speech, what they're really demanding is "consequence-free" free speech—the freedom to cause harm to others without bearing responsibility for what they've said. They try to pass such harm as jokes or mere intellectual debate, but when speech is used to denigrate people's identities to reinforce a hierarchy of unfair power relationships, this provides a teachable moment for students to learn the difference between brave spaces and safe spaces. In "brave" spaces, you say what you want and take responsibility for saying it. In "safe" spaces, you either hide what you want to say, or hope that no one seeks to hold you accountable if you say something problematic."

—LORETTA ROSS

# Creating a Sustainable Practice: Student Ownership

Facilitation can be exhausting, and we have to remember that our goal is for students to have ownership of their own learning. Ultimately, students shouldn't need your guidance to have a conversation. There will not always be an adult to remind them of tools and strategies. Making sure that you are modeling how to facilitate is key, but so is gradually releasing responsibility.

## How Do I Know If It's Working?

One of my favorite ways to dialogue is to invite students to participate in a Circle, which is rooted in Indigenous and First Nations cultures and practices. This process ensures that community members are heard, and that those who wish to speak are able to do so without interruption. In a Circle, an item of significance is chosen as a talking piece, and when the talking piece is in someone's hands, it is their turn to speak. Students take turns leading different sections, such as introducing the Circle, posing a question, and closing the Circle. Try to create a routine for holding Circles in your class so that students can take turns deciding on the question or topic for discussion.

Here are some basic guidelines for a Talking Circle from the *BC First Nations Land, Title, and Governance Teacher Resource Guide* (First Nations Education Steering Committee 2019):

>> The group sits in a circle, so everyone can see each other.

>> One person introduces the topic for discussion (often the leader of the group).

>> Only the person holding the special object speaks; everyone else listens respectfully giving the speaker their full attention.

>> Everyone is given a chance to speak, but someone may pass the object without speaking if they wish.

>> Speakers use "I" statements, stating what they are thinking or feeling, rather than commenting on what other people have said.

>> Once everyone has had a chance to speak, the object can be passed around again giving people a chance to continue the discussion.

## Don't Reinvent the Wheel

There are a myriad of books and articles in the world about how to speak up or facilitate, but no matter how much information you consume, you will only grow more comfortable and confident with practice. Remember that you don't learn how to cook just by reading cookbooks. You have to start cooking in the kitchen.

>> *Courageous Conversations About Race*, by Glenn E. Singleton

>> *Let's Talk*, from Learning for Justice. https://www.learning forjustice.org/magazine/publications/lets-talk

>> *Speak Up at School*, from Learning for Justice. https://www .learningforjustice.org/magazine/publications/speak-up-at-school

>> *Our Words, Our Ways: Teaching First Nations, Métis and Inuit Learners.* https://education.alberta.ca/media/3615876/our -words-our-ways.pdf

>> First Nations Pedagogy Online. www.firstnationspedagogy.ca

>> *The Art of Gathering* by Priya Parker

>> *The Little Book of Restorative Justice in Education: Fostering Responsibility, Healing, and Hope in Schools* by Katherine Evans and Dorothy Vaandering

>> *Nonviolent Communication* by Marshall B. Rosenberg

# { 4 }

# How Can I Work with Parents and Caregivers?

START HERE

**IN MY FIRST FEW YEARS OF TEACHING,** I planned a unit on gender stereotyping for my third-grade class. Over a few weeks, we studied toy marketing based on gender, analyzed gender role stereotypes in fairy tales, and examined the roles of boys and girls in some of the picture books in our classroom library. I was proud of the progress students made in these lessons, and even more pleased that the kids were noticing gender biases in the movies and TV shows they watched at home. One day, I received an email from a concerned family about a book I read to my class called *Jacob's New Dress* by Ian and Sarah Hoffman (2014). The story centers around a young boy who feels more comfortable wearing a dress to school and searches for acceptance and support from his peers.

This family's email was not angry or laden with profanity. They stated that due to their religious beliefs, they did not want their child exposed to any LGBTQ+ topics, nor did they support conversations around gender identity or expression in the classroom. In the end, they asked that in the future their child be removed from lessons on this topic. Naively, I was caught off guard. My former school is located in Los Angeles, has a very upfront commitment to diversity, and has a number of LGBTQ-identifying families and staff members. I responded politely, thanked them for communicating their concerns, and told them that their child would be given an alternative activity during future conversations.

In hindsight, I am ashamed of how I responded. Even as a self-identifying queer person, I failed to be an accomplice to my own community. I centered the comfort of these parents more than I dared to stand up for my LGBTQ+ students, friends, colleagues, and myself. Naturally, I've replayed this scenario imagining all the things I should have said. I could have pushed back. I could have asked for more information or defended my decision to teach about gender inclusivity. What prevented me from taking a different course of action? Fear of rocking the boat and inciting anger from this family.

For many of my peers, this fear is very real. We worry that certain community members will undermine our work; we worry about losing our standing in the school; we worry about alienating ourselves from our colleagues. In independent schools, charter schools, and public school districts with unions that hold little power, there is also fear of losing our job. The fear can be so intense that we either don't address ABAR work in our classrooms or we do so in ways that avoid detection.

# Setting Yourself Up for Success: Seek to Understand and Communicate

Rather than avoiding caregivers due to the fear of retaliation, we can take steps to engage them as partners in our social justice work. Family and caregiver engagement is a crucial piece of student success. Ideally, schools, teachers, and caregivers would work in perfect harmony to support students. However, in the media these days there are far too many stories from both caregivers and teachers, each lamenting the damage they believe the other is causing to the child. These stresses on the school–home relationship chip away at the trust and respect that need to be in place in order for teachers to do their best teaching, and to help students learn.

When we engage with caregivers we can start to understand and address some of their valid concerns. I recently asked a number of families to share their experiences, thoughts, and concerns on social justice topics being covered in the classroom. Here's what I learned:

> *It's difficult as a parent to know when your child is developmentally ready to process tragic injustice in the world. I worry my child does not have the communication tools or comfort level to reach out for additional support.*

> *I might worry about a teacher's personal views on things like politics or religion coming into play.*

> *I don't want my child to feel ashamed for being white, or to feel like the villain in history.*

Each of these family members makes an important and valid point. I would never want my own child to be ostracized for having a viewpoint that differs from the majority or for their teacher to preach a personal agenda. While some might assume that white caregivers are the primary objectors to issues of race and equity being discussed in the classroom, parents of color also voice concerns about how teachers would navigate these topics.

> *I might be worried that my kid may be bullied for expressing beliefs that his classmates disagree with.*

> *My son is Black, and I don't want him to feel uncomfortable or tokenized because there aren't many Black students in the class or school. I remember being the only Black kid in class and my teacher putting me on the spot when we talked about slavery. It was humiliating.*

> *As a parent of color, one of the biggest concerns I have is how much work the teacher has done BEFORE ever bringing up race and justice in the classroom. Have they worked with professionals in confronting their own biases? Do they notice if they "favor" white children in language and classroom management?*

Recently, I spoke with a Black father who shared that one of his young children had been involved in a racial incident at school. He was alarmed when the parent of one of the other students involved called to apologize, because he had no warning or context. He had not received any notifications from his child's teacher about what occurred. When he reached out to the teacher, she tried to assure him, "We talked about it. Everything is fine." This did not sit well with him. He explained he deeply believes that young students need to be educated about race and racism; what upset him was that he was left out of the conversation and had to learn about a potentially harmful incident involving his daughter from another parent. He was skeptical of the teacher's ability to lead a conversation around race with students when the teacher clearly was not comfortable communicating about these issues with adults.

Caregivers must be a part of the conversation, especially if their child is involved in an incident regarding an issue of bias or racism. There are many situations that require educators to dig into their own identity work, unpack their biases, and expand their lens to understand why a parent such as this Black father was rattled by this interaction. Even if you are recently embarking on your understanding of social justice topics and equity in education, take ownership of where you are along the spectrum. It's also important to note that family members such as this father typically don't object to social justice topics being taught in the classroom; rather, they worry about *how* the conversations and lessons are approached.

So where do we start? Before you begin any social justice unit, there are things every teacher can do to improve family communication and engagement.

## } KEEP IN MIND {

"You have to practice talking about race and being uncomfortable. Having adult conversations with antiracist teachers is key. Having vulnerable conversations with parents is key. Having classroom discussions with children where you listen to them is key because that allows you to become less uncomfortable. It's OK to have uncomfortable experiences."

—KELLY BROWN (HE/HIM)

## Family Survey

At the beginning of the year, I like to send home a survey like the one in Figure 4–1 for all family members in my class. The purpose is to gain insight into my students' lives outside of school, but the most useful question to me is "What are your memories of learning as a child?" I have received multiple paragraph responses from families, some lauding their favorite grade school memories, others reliving trauma from authoritarian teachers who chipped away at their self-esteem. Gaining an understanding of caregivers' educational experiences provides insight into how they may view you as a teacher, and whether they may be carrying any baggage. For example, if a family member attended a school where textbooks were outdated and teachers suppressed student voices, they might be skeptical that you have the ability to foster their child's identity and experiences in a positive way. For white families, there may be a fear that their child may be shamed, and for families of color, that their child may be tokenized or taught only how people like them have been oppressed. When we understand caregivers' experiences, we are able to support them in proactive ways.

Dear Parents and Family Members,

In order for us to best work with your child, please complete the following questionnaire.

Student's name:_____

What are your academic and socio-emotional goals for your student this year? (Please be as specific as possible)

What was your experience like in this grade? How do you remember school?

What are your fears or concerns about your child this year in school, if any?

What does your child enjoy doing outside of school?

What does a typical after school afternoon/evening look like in your home?

What motivates your child? What triggers your child?

Next June, what do you hope your child says about his/her experience in this class? What's the story you hope he/she/they will tell?

What method of communication works best for your family?

Which languages are spoken in your home?

Please feel free to share any additional information about your student or family:

**FIGURE 4–1** Sample Caregiver Survey

## Give Caregivers a Heads-Up and Follow Up with Support

Alerting families to upcoming topics that will be covered in class is not the same as asking permission. To me, asking permission often feels like I'm implying that I'm doing something wrong, and there is nothing wrong with discussing issues stemming from bias or racism in schools. In my experience, families do not like being taken by surprise, especially when it comes to their children. Before starting a unit on a topic that could be considered divisive, I like to send out a communication to all families and caregivers in my class. For example, before and after the student walkout following the Parkland school shooting, I sent this to my classroom community:

### (Before)

*Dear parents and caregivers,*

*Our students are 9 and 10 years old, so a big concern for me has been whether or not they can articulate WHY they're participating in the walkout (rather than viewing it as an extended recess or time to hang with their friends outside). This morning's prompt asked the kids to explain why they are walking out if they choose to do so. I was impressed with their reflections, and the passion they conveyed in their writing. We emphasized that this is 100% optional, and our teaching assistant will be remaining inside if students do not want to participate.*

*As we're an elementary school, our walkout will be held outside classrooms within our campus, and students will be participating in restorative justice circles to reflect on safety in our community. We'll also spend time studying different protests in history, and make signs that can be used in future protests. Please don't hesitate to reach out if you have any questions or concerns.*

*Warmly,*

*Ms. Liz*

### (After)

*Hi parents and caregivers,*

*The walkout today went smoothly as planned. The majority of our class chose to participate, and some chose to remain inside. Those who joined in held a restorative justice circle outside, and shared extremely powerful thoughts and feelings about current events in our school and community. As we brought the discussion back inside, we talked about safe schools, and what we can do to make our community an inclusive space.*

*We also had a lesson on protests (what is a protest, what types of protest are there, and why people protest) and read a book about how students took the lead on the desegregation of businesses in Savannah during the Civil Rights Movement. We also made signs for future protests, as some mentioned they plan on attending the March for Our Lives on March 24th.*

*I've attached a few photos for you to see examples of our work from today, as well as some links to additional resources to support your kiddos at home and continue today's conversations. Thank you all for your love and support!*

*Warmly,*

*Ms. Liz*

It was important to me that the caregivers knew how the day was planned, and what their child could expect when they arrived in the morning. Additionally, as we understand that families are our partners in this work, it is crucial to point them in the direction of books, articles, and research to support their child's academic and social–emotional learning.

## Communicate and Be Transparent

I remember many repetitive conversations on car rides home and at the dinner table with my parents. They would ask, "How was school today?" and I would say, "Fine." They would ask, "What did you do?" and I would mix it up with replies of either "I don't remember" or "I don't know, stuff." This went on for years.

Many caregivers feel frustrated because they don't know what is happening in their child's classroom. Additionally, many students pick and choose parts of conversations to share at home that may not reflect the whole lesson.

Every year, I create a private Facebook group for families in my classroom. In this group, I repost school communications that go out in flyers and emails, but I also post photos of anchor charts, student work, and parts of lessons. Figure 4–2 shows one post and a response from a parent. I try to post at least once a day, so family members have conversation starters with their kids at the end of the day. I share photos that represent a range of student work and the sequence of the lesson. If families do not use social media, I'll send a separate email or letter with a few sentences letting them know what we discussed and how their student contributed. If you create a social media page for your class, you *must* get consent from parents and caregivers before photographing students or including any identifiable student information (school media release forms do not grant teachers permission to post on their personal social media accounts). While social media is an effective way to engage families, do spend time beforehand familiarizing yourself with the Family Educational Rights and Privacy Act (FERPA). This is a federal law that protects students' privacy by giving families control over information that may personally identify their student. It also allows parents access to their child's educational records. For more information, check out https://studentprivacy.ed.gov/.

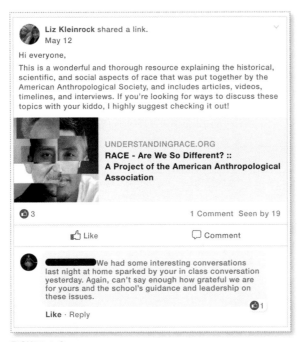

**FIGURE 4–2** Sample Class Facebook Group Post and Parent Response

{ KEEP IN MIND }

"They [parents, caregivers and students] understand things about their own experiences and their own lives, and their own education that you don't understand. As the teacher, you need to approach it with some humility and be open to learning and listening instead of thinking that you have all the answers. All teachers, but especially white teachers, need to think about how to de-center ourselves and our individual experiences, and remind ourselves that what we've experienced doesn't hold true for everyone else."

—CHARLIE McGEEHAN (HE/HIM)

# Taking Action in the Classroom: Cultivate Community

My first principal, a huge advocate for community-building, would constantly remind the staff, "We can always go back and reteach a lesson, but community is the one thing we cannot afford to get wrong." I love using the book *Thank You, Mr. Falker,* by Patricia Polacco (1998), to discuss what makes an effective teacher while my class lists good teacher qualities and steps teachers should take to support their students. As you read this, you may be well into the school year, but it's important to reflect and determine what you can do to cultivate community with students and families.

## Create a Roles and Responsibilities Chart with Students and Families

During the first weeks of school, I dedicate an enormous amount of time to building community with both students and families. At Back-to-School Night, I ask families in my class to add to a Roles and Responsibilities chart my students started during the first weeks of school. This is a helpful way to launch the partnership between home and school. It sets the foundation for accountability between the student, teacher, and family. Family members add to the chart reflections on their role in supporting their student, describing what this looks like in the home environment. Families and caregivers can read what their children have written and think about how teachers and caregivers can create a joint system to support the learning and social–emotional development of students. Figure 4–3 shows a completed chart with the roles of teachers, students, and caregivers.

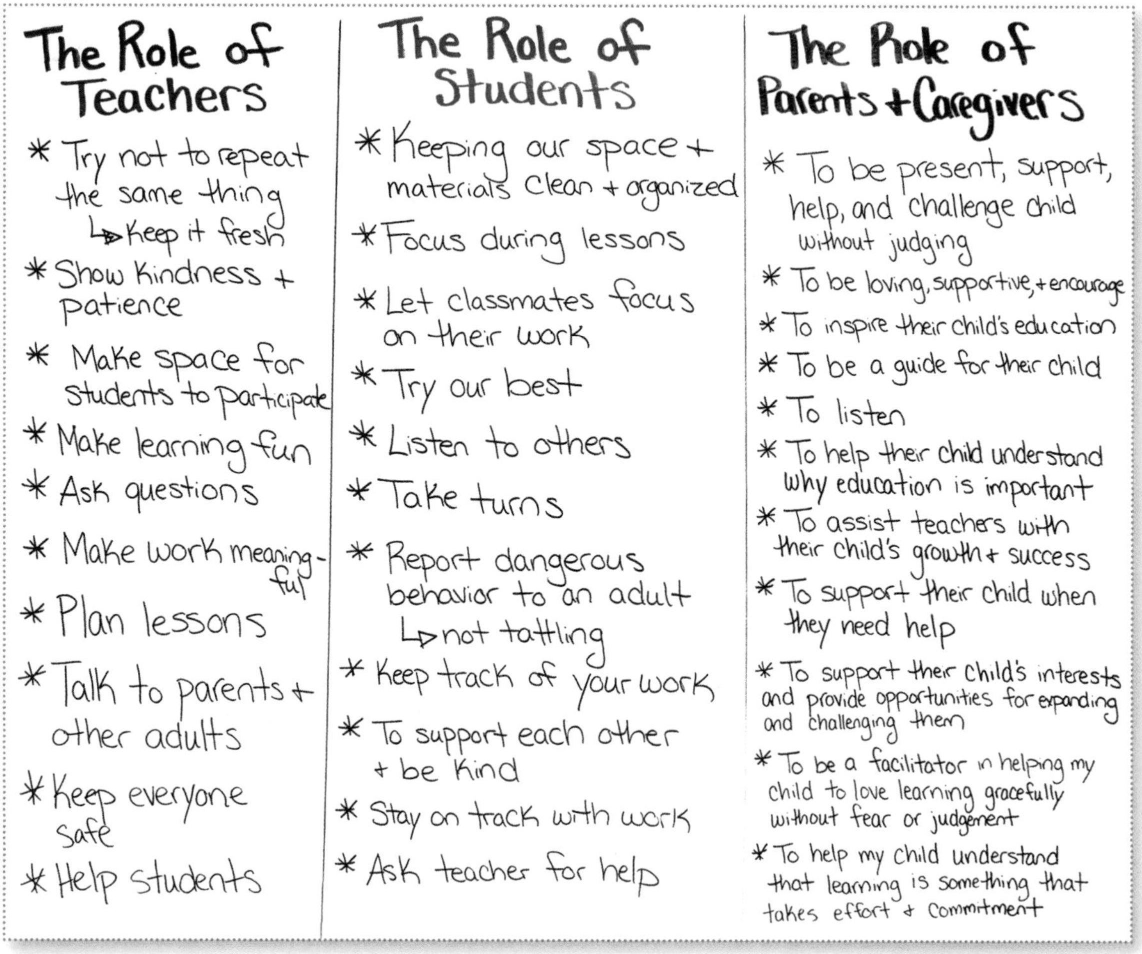

## The Role of Teachers

* Try not to repeat the same thing
  ↳ Keep it fresh
* Show kindness + patience
* Make space for students to participate
* Make learning fun
* Ask questions
* Make work meaning-ful
* Plan lessons
* Talk to parents + other adults
* Keep everyone safe
* Help students

## The Role of Students

* Keeping our space + materials clean + organized
* Focus during lessons
* Let classmates focus on their work
* Try our best
* Listen to others
* Take turns
* Report dangerous behavior to an adult
  ↳ not tattling
* Keep track of your work
* To support each other + be kind
* Stay on track with work
* Ask teacher for help

## The Role of Parents + Caregivers

* To be present, support, help, and challenge child without judging
* To be loving, supportive, + encourage
* To inspire their child's education
* To be a guide for their child
* To listen
* To help their child understand why education is important
* To assist teachers with their child's growth + success
* To support their child when they need help
* To support their child's interests and provide opportunities for expanding and challenging them
* To be a facilitator in helping my child to love learning gracefully without fear or judgement
* To help my child understand that learning is something that takes effort + commitment

FIGURE 4–3 A Completed Roles and Responsibilities chart

## Collect Data

When you've built up comfort in creating lessons and units that address issues of bias or racism, inviting families to participate can be a powerful learning tool for both students and adults. A few years ago I wrote a unit about the origin of race. I started by asking students how comfortable they felt talking about race.

My students anonymously ranked themselves on a scale from 1 to 5, and wrote a few sentences explaining their score. Based on my students' inquiries on the subject, we then identified what we knew upon beginning the unit, what questions we hoped to answer throughout our study, and what new understandings we had gained (commonly called a *KWL chart*, these track what students "Know," "Want to know," and "Learned"). From the left, Figure 4–4 shows our KWL chart and my students' self-identified comfort levels. I created the same survey online and sent it to my students' families. Figure 4–5 displays the compiled

A

### Exploring the Concept of Race

| KNOW | WANT TO KNOW | LEARNED |
|---|---|---|
| -Can connect to your skin color | -Why did people want to separate others? | -The US had/has laws that allow(ed) racial discrimination |
| -People get hurt b/c of their race | -Why do some discriminate based on race? ✓ | -Thomas Jefferson had a huge impact on race |
| -Race was created to differentiate people | -When did racial discrimination begin | -Dehumanization of people of color, negative stereotypes |
| -Skin color comes from where your ancestors lived (melanin) | -Where does race come from? | -People used science to support racism |
| -Sometimes used to dehumanize | -Why was race invented? | -Use of images, cartoons, media to promote racism |
| -People of all races can be allies | -What would the world be like w/out race? | -Race was invented based on visible differences |

FIGURE 4–4A–B A KWL chart exploring the concept of race and a bar chart showing students' comfort level when talking about race

B

How comfortable do you feel talking about RACE?

1  2  3  4  5

parents' and family members' responses to the same question: "On a scale from 1 to 5, how comfortable are you talking about race and racism?" In class we compared and contrasted the data from adults and students and reflected on what we learned. It was a powerful learning experience for students to see that the adults in their lives held the same concerns and fears that they themselves had expressed in class.

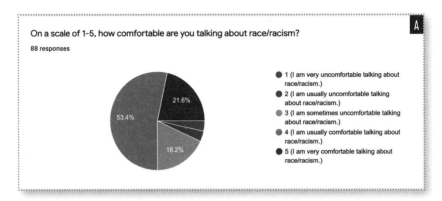

**On a scale of 1-5, how comfortable are you talking about race/racism?**

88 responses

21.6%

53.4%

18.2%

- ● 1 (I am very uncomfortable talking about race/racism.)
- ● 2 (I am usually uncomfortable talking about race/racism.)
- ● 3 (I am sometimes uncomfortable talking about race/racism.)
- ● 4 (I am usually comfortable talking about race/racism.)
- ● 5 (I am very comfortable talking about race/racism.)

**If possible, please give an explanation or any additional details for your answer.**

43 responses

I am very comfortable being in conversations about race/racism. I sometimes feel uncomfortable when I want to speak, not because the topics make me uncomfortable, but because I think I don't have as much experience/education as I'd like with the specific terms used to discuss race/racism. I know what I want to say but I have a harder time articulating than I would like. I think this could be because I didn't actually start talking about race until I got into college.

We are a mixed family with many different countries behind us, so it is part of our everyday life.

As a white male, it can be uncomfortable to confront the fact that you propagate and benefit from a racist system. Also, it sucks when you want to say something, but because you don't have a lived experience or certain background your contribution to the conversation is discounted or sometimes you get in trouble for talking.

In my own perpective, I don't mind talking about races as well as racism. Though in many countries racism is normal in which people tend to talk anytime. Talking about races, where you came from is a very humble doing.

Sometimes I am afraid I will say the wrong thing. For instance, I asked someone recently if they were Vietnamese and they were Chinese. They thought if was funny but it showed my ignorance. Is that racist?

**FIGURE 4–5A–B** Family Responses to "How Comfortable Are You Talking About Race, and Why?"

## Create a Sign-Up for Mystery Readers, Guest Teachers, and Classroom Volunteers

Throughout the year, search for opportunities to invite families into the classroom to become part of the learning community. I like to offer both paper and online sign-ups for family members to be Mystery Readers at a set time each week, and a different parent will choose a book and surprise the class with a read-aloud. While this does not always address issues around teaching with an ABAR lens, it does provide adults a valuable snapshot of your classroom environment—which can build trust between home and school.

## Check for Understanding and Misunderstanding

A few years ago, while my class was learning about protests and Black Lives Matter, I received an email from a parent. She explained that her son had come home and, when asked what he learned in school that day, said, "We learned about why police officers are bad." The mother also shared that they had police officers in their family and wanted clarity on the classroom conversation. I wrote back and explained that we had been learning about protests and bias, and had discussed what happens when people in positions of power act on their biases and end up hurting others. There was mutual understanding after this exchange, but it also reminded me that it was my responsibility to make sure my students hadn't misinterpreted any new concepts. After every lesson or conversation, make sure there are ample opportunities for students to process and reflect and for you to gauge understanding. You can give students time to write in journals and share their thinking with a partner or group; ask students to write what they learned on sticky notes, pass them around, and/or post them in a public area of the classroom; and conduct community circles so students with different communication styles can express themselves. While you'll want to use this time to check for understanding, this is also an important opportunity to check for students' *mis*understandings.

# Creating a Sustainable Practice: Partnerships for Joint Learning

Let's assume that a few weeks or months have gone by since your first ABAR lesson or unit with your class. Some families have expressed apprehension about how the conversations will be introduced to their children, but you've maintained transparent communication to ease concerns and you feel confident that your students gained valuable take-aways. While it is easy to breathe a sigh of relief and plunge onward in this work, keep in mind that two-way communication with families will continue to be a key component in maintaining sustainability.

## How Do I Know If It's Working? Checking In with Caregivers

Some initiatives to build community and trust with caregivers will be more successful than others. All communities have different dominant cultural, political, and religious beliefs, and there is no "one size fits all" when it comes to family and caregiver engagement. Rather than viewing family engagement as a series of separate interactions, ask yourself, "How does each communication build upon previous interactions in order to establish trust and mutual respect?"

Use the assessment template in Figure 4–6 to monitor communication between school and home, and to track the effectiveness of different outreach strategies.

Sample reflection questions:

>> How have I built trust, and made families and caregivers a part of our classroom community?

>> How have I created opportunities for caregivers to participate?

>> What work have I done to communicate and include caregivers in the learning process?

>> What is the nature of my communication with a specific student's family? Is it one of celebration or correction?

OR 4–1

Family and Caregiver Engagement Assessment

| | |
|---|---|
| **Reflection question:** | |
| **Specific actions** | |
| **What happened?** (Be as objective as possible.) | |
| **Reactions** (me, students, families, colleagues, administration, friends) | |
| **Reason for reaction** (Did I seek to understand where the other party is coming from? What information did I gain that can affect my practice?) | |
| **Refinement** (What can I change to improve this work?) | |

© 2021 by Liz Kleinroth, from Start Here, Start Now. Portsmouth, NH: Heinemann.

FIGURE 4–6 Family and Caregiver Engagement Assessment

>> Do I share about myself to my students' families and caregivers? Do they know who I am beyond the classroom?

>> How am I including families and caregivers who speak languages other than English?

>> How do I engage with families and caregivers that I know hold different beliefs or come from backgrounds different from my own? How can I seek to understand where they're coming from?

## Don't Reinvent the Wheel

Some educators may hold the identity of teacher and parent or care-giver, and some may not have the experience of knowing what it's like to raise a child. Even if you have your own young learners at home, "parent" or "caregiver" is not a monolithic term, and there are many resources available that speak to engaging different home communities.

>> *Engage Every Family*, by Steven M. Constantino

>> *Building Culturally Responsive Family–School Relationships*, by Ellen S. Amatea

>> "Planting the Seeds for a New World: Cultivating an Anti-Bias, Anti-Racist Home," by Razan Abdin-Adnani (*AMI/USA Journal*, Spring 2018)

>> *Critical Practices for Anti-bias Education: Family and Community Engagement*, from Learning for Justice

>> *Beyond the Bake Sale: The Essential Guide to Family–School Partnerships*, by Anne T. Henderson, Karen L. Mapp, Vivian R. Johnson, and Don Davies

>> *Powerful Partnerships: A Teacher's Guide to Engaging Families for Student Success*, by Karen L. Mapp, Ilene Carver, and Jessica Lander

>> *Sitting in the Fire: Large Group Transformation Using Conflict and Diversity*, by Arnold Mindell

>> *The Art of Gathering: How We Meet and Why It Matters*, by Priya Parker

# { 5 }

# How Can I Partner with My Administration to Support ABAR Work?

START HERE

**A FEW YEARS AGO,** I was approached by a teacher while facilitating a workshop on teaching about the Holocaust. She shared that she had been a classroom teacher for more than thirty years, loved her students, and was passionate about teaching history from multiple perspectives. In recent years, she had begun to learn more about the Holocaust and antisemitism and wanted to integrate this knowledge into her lessons and planning. This did not sit well with her principal, who told her that teaching about the Holocaust was too political and, since it wasn't part of the mandated curriculum, she would be terminated if these practices continued. As we spoke, she shared that she had recently made the decision to retire early rather than continue to work in an environment where teaching about history and injustice could lead to being fired.

I spoke to approximately a dozen teachers who had faced pushback from their principal or school leadership over teaching about diverse identities and history. In some cases, like that of the teacher who taught about the Holocaust, the interactions between teacher and administration were openly hostile. With others, the pushback came in the form of radio silence or the absence of support (remember that silence is also a political message). One teacher who read a book about a transgender character was left to face an angry parent who didn't want their child "being indoctrinated." This teacher felt embarrassed and defeated when their principal moved the student into a different classroom. Another teacher was reprimanded for teaching about enslavement and was told to "keep politics out of the classroom." In each situation, similar justifications were given by school leaders: the lesson was too partisan, too divisive, not part of the curriculum, and took time away from teaching other subjects.

In some cases, school leaders may be under the impression that they *are* doing effective and meaningful ABAR work, yet such initiatives must be scrutinized for surface-level performativity and for whether or not they are based on deficit ideologies. In his article "Avoiding Racial Equity Detours," Equity Literacy Institute and EdChange founder Paul Gorski (2019) (he/him) outlines a series of common pitfalls. These are school-administered strategies that may create the illusion of progress by appearing to include or advocate for marginalized students. For example, a school might host an annual Diversity Day celebration, while ignoring systemic problems that harm BIPOC and LGBTQ+ students. Or the school might champion cultural competence without directly addressing racism or the prevalence of white supremacist culture. In a follow-up conversation, Gorski also describes the "Shiny New Thing" detour, where schools latch on to specific programs like Mindfulness, Social–Emotional Learning, or Restorative Justice. The holistic perspective of these programs does benefit students, but does not challenge the systems that harm and exclude. Taking deep breaths when stressed or naming emotions are important skills, but these will neither help teachers dismantle their biases nor push a principal to consider how a school policy discriminates against a particular demographic.

Before moving forward, it's important to recognize and acknowledge the nuances of school leadership, culture, and accountability. Decisions that impact teachers and students do not begin and end with principals and assistant principals. It's possible to have a school leadership team that is incredibly supportive of ABAR work but operates under a heavily resistant school board or other governing body. There are also principals who may commit to having your back verbally, but who fail to show up in practice when someone in the community pushes back. While classroom teachers can certainly impact the culture of a school, there are often structural issues that cannot be resolved by one person. These problems exist because they are systemic in nature. They require the redistribution of power within the organization. Classroom educators have a responsibility to participate in this work and advocate for more inclusive and equitable learning environments; however, systemic work and shifting a community's culture takes time.

The purpose of this chapter is to identify the ways in which educators can work with school leaders to teach from an ABAR lens, and to address any perceived lack of support for ABAR implementation from administrators or school leaders who are wary of how it may be executed in the classroom. My hope is to shed light on how to navigate these conversations from a proactive and action-based approach, as well as to provide insight into the experiences and perspectives of administrators who support their teachers in ABAR work.

I also want to note the challenge and struggle of holding multiple truths that I experienced while writing and editing this chapter. I would not call this section of my book revolutionary. When I discuss standards-based alignment, I am constantly reminded of my friend Dr. Dena Simmons (she/her) and how she pushed me to see that standardization of academics inherently marginalizes students of certain identities. When working with students, it's a balance of teaching them *how* to navigate systems that currently exist for their own survival, while also pushing them to think *beyond* the systems that exist and what dismantling and rebuilding them could look like. While I believe in pushing for rethinking and reconstructing education in the United States, the strategies in this chapter fall into the former category because teachers need to navigate the system in order to mitigate harm done to students as quickly as possible. If you feel that you are beyond what I have written in this chapter, I encourage you to explore the work of the Abolitionist Teaching Network at www.abolitionistteachingnetwork.org.

Lastly, I recognize the privileged position I hold as an outsider to you, the reader, as I encourage you to push boundaries and challenge the status quo. For those who work in schools or districts without the strength of unions or protective contracts, or in places where a teacher can instantly be deemed ineffective and blacklisted, or fired due to their

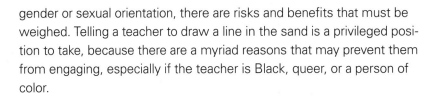

gender or sexual orientation, there are risks and benefits that must be weighed. Telling a teacher to draw a line in the sand is a privileged position to take, because there are a myriad reasons that may prevent them from engaging, especially if the teacher is Black, queer, or a person of color.

# Setting Yourself Up for Success: Gathering Perspective

One of the most enjoyable experiences of writing this book was learning from a variety of public, charter, and independent school leaders. When I began drafting preliminary interview questions, I immediately realized that, despite my years of classroom experience and working in schools, I had no idea what it's like to be a principal. I had no idea how principals spend their days, what they worry about, and how teachers are unaware of many aspects of operating a school.

When you're hired as a classroom teacher, your realm of responsibilities is fairly clear: instructing students, planning and preparing lessons, grading, communicating with families, and possible additional requirements like supervising lunch and recess, or leading a club or coaching a sports team. (This list does not include additional roles teachers end up taking on without financial compensation, such as mentoring, providing resources, emotionally supporting students and families.) Principals and assistant principals wear multiple hats, many of which are swapped on and off throughout one school day. Principal Scott Thomas (he/him) in Minnesota reflected on the responsibilities of school leaders that can often leave them feeling pulled in different directions. "I think that sometimes teachers don't realize that we are constantly facing competing agendas from all sides. There are multiple outcomes we have to be focused on at the same time. There's a lot that we keep from our teachers too because we want to protect them and don't want them to know how ugly things are at times. I share a lot with my teachers but sharing every negative thing that's going on isn't going to be helpful." Jessie Elliot (she/her), administrative director and a founder of a small, independent, Waldorf-inspired school in California, agreed and noted that administrators also need to be constantly mindful of the layers of confidentiality around topics related to specific students and finance. "As administrators, we hold the general health and well-being of the school, which is sort of like having a parent or being a parent. If the school is sick, we're the ones who are aware and we're trying to find ways to make it better. But we don't want to walk around talking about how sick the school is, because it can cause people to panic." Principals may also be the most visible leaders and decision-makers of a school. However, assistant principal and consultant Jamilah Pitts (she/her) reminds those outside of this role to broaden their understanding of the system in which each school exists. "An administrator may sit at the forefront of a school, but if they're in a network of schools, they have to report to their deputy superintendent who refers to the superintendent and then the school board. Sometimes there's a huge hierarchy or chain of command that principals have to report to even if they're the person who is supposed to be sitting at the forefront of the school. We often have to shift or navigate these systems in different ways."

There's also a perception that people in leadership positions hold more knowledge than other employees, so they must have the answers to difficult-to-answer problems. As simple as this may sound, school administrators are just as human and prone to self-doubt and uncertainty as any teacher. No one wants to be judged as someone who doesn't understand issues surrounding diversity or antiracism. Administrators are fearful of using the wrong language, offending people in the community, being misunderstood, and hearing the angry parent on the phone demanding to know why the school is forcing a political agenda on their children. If school leaders are not experienced in having challenging conversations or developing fluency around ABAR either in their own lives or within the school community, it's easy to see how these attitudes and behaviors can trickle down to faculty and staff.

## Build a Coalition of Stakeholders

In earlier chapters, I emphasized the importance of finding fellow supporters for the purpose of building large-scale capacity for this work. If there are like-minded staff members at your school, even in different grade levels or departments, how can you work together? Form a partnership around an activity, unit, or culminating event. Some of my favorite ABAR-focused units included collaborating with an art teacher as my students studied the art and writing of Faith Ringgold. Another was working with the second-grade teacher to arrange a visit from my fourth graders, who had written speeches about the importance of being an upstander instead of a bystander. If your school leadership is resistant, having a partner in the room feels drastically different from facing your principal alone.

Families and caregivers are also incredible assets. They often raise powerful voices when it comes to addressing the needs of a school. How can they support you? Perhaps families and caregivers can

>> email your school administration in support of ABAR work

>> ask to be included in stakeholder meetings

>> collaborate with teachers (especially if your school has a director of diversity or a diversity committee) to organize parent and caregiver workshops or book clubs to support ABAR at home

>> interview other families of diverse backgrounds about their experiences at the school, and how inclusion efforts can be improved.

Together, partnerships between teachers and caregivers further support the case for how ABAR must be ingrained in the culture of your school, as there are shared values between school and home.

## { KEEP IN MIND }

"Find colleagues who also want to engage in the work and do it together. One of the central flaws of teachers is trying to do everything by yourself, which can also connect to having a white savior complex. I think working with other people is key. That means finding other white people who also want to engage in the work and who are willing to read and study with you. Reach out to colleagues of color to see how you can support them. It's not the job of people of color to educate white people about their experiences. We can't just be isolated as white people doing this work."

—CHARLIE McGEEHAN (HE/HIM)

## Find the Root of the Concern

In any situation that requires problem-solving, we have to identify the root of your administrator's concern. You can start by thinking about your unique school community. The language and methods teachers utilize may differ depending on the type of school and its stakeholders. For example, one principal may be more concerned with how tuition-paying family members push back, while another may be focused on teachers aligning their lessons with standards or preparing their students for standardized assessments. Some school leaders may be under pressure from the superintendent or board members. Being able to identify the cause of your administrator's reluctance or skepticism will guide you in making an actionable plan that reflects your understanding of their position, and how you plan to directly address their concerns. In Figure 5–1, I offer some possible if–then scenarios.

FIGURE 5–1 If–Then Scenarios

| If | Then |
| --- | --- |
| **The concern is a matter of trust . . .** | Determine how you can demonstrate transparency to show that you can facilitate these conversations in a respectful and appropriate way, such as inviting your administrator to your classroom to observe a lesson. |
| **The concern is a matter of external pressure . . .** | Determine how you can use multiple voices in the school community to advocate for your cause. Many schools hold public board meetings or town hall events. Can you organize people to show up and support the cause? |
| **The concern is a matter of caregiver reactions . . .** | Determine why caregivers are pushing back, and brainstorm ways to involve them in this work (see Chapter 3). Can you work with your administration to host an ABAR workshop for parents and families? |
| **The concern is a personal challenge . . .** | Remember "connection before correction." Can you connect with them by sharing your own growth as an ABAR educator, and the steps you took? Are there resources you can share? |

## Do Your Homework and Make a Plan You Can Defend

In some cases, administrators might be more concerned with how certain topics will be introduced and taught rather than with the topic itself. When planning for a meeting or discussion to advocate for ABAR in your classroom, come up with an action plan that is not only clear and academically aligned, but that you can also defend every step of the way. If you're approaching apprehensive administration, Natalie Randolph (she/her), Director of Equity, Justice & Community at an independent school in Washington, DC, advises teachers to develop a plan and prepare different iterations of that plan, to show that you've put in an enormous amount of thought and energy and are mindful of its execution. "Focus on what's under your control," Randolph reminds. "What is under your control is mapping it out as best you can so that it's very difficult to say no. Try not to get hung up on the mere morality of it, like everybody should do this, everybody should do the right thing to do. Sometimes we forget about the fact that that's not how anybody persuades anybody else to do anything. Like this whole world is built on persuading folks to buy something or to buy into something and as much as we believe that equity and justice work is like completely outside of that, it works the exact same way. You need to market it to your school and you need to show people what the benefits are, and you need to reach people who might not agree with you and change their mind."

If you're thinking about creating a proposal for your administrator, your plans should reflect the care and intention that you bring to this work in the classroom. Before you request an in-person meeting to share your ideas, reflect on the following questions:

>> How will I ensure that this lesson or unit aligns with our academic focus?

>> Is my lesson aligned with standards, and if so, which ones?

>> What texts and resources will I use?

>> What are the academic and ABAR goals?

>> How will I communicate our work with parents and caregivers?

>> What is the sequence of the lesson or unit? What foundational knowledge do my students already have? What is the objective?

>> How will I check for student understanding?

>> What outside resources will support my students? What trainings or professional development opportunities are available to support my own education?

>> What evidence can I provide that shows I know this content and who my students are in the event that something problematic occurs?

>> Am I aware of my biases? How will I respond if I'm accused of pushing my own agenda?

By considering and preparing answers to these questions, you may be able to address any concerns your administrator has. You'll also be able to show them that you've thought about your plan from different angles.

## Build Trust

In the not-so-distant past, a friend of mine asked me to talk to her head of school about prioritizing ABAR professional development for the staff. The teachers had requested it and her principal was advocating for it. The final obstacle was the one white school leader with the power to have the final say. This head of school finally agreed, but it was clear that her resistance stemmed from her own insecurity. During our consultation, she balked at the idea of discussing gender with students. She assured me that the school would support nonbinary or transgender students, but they didn't have any, so why should they talk about it? (I reminded her that her school in fact does have trans and nonbinary students, but the reason they don't know might be because there is no evidence that the school is a safe environment, so students are not comfortable sharing their identities). She also asked if I would be available on retainer to write diversity statements and help her respond to concerned parents. While I did end up facilitating one day of workshops with the staff, I declined the offer to be her personal ABAR fixer.

This particular head of school is an example of a gatekeeper, or someone who single-handedly prevents the progress of a community. Often this reflects larger systemic issues within an organization, as decision-making power should not lie within a single person. That is why it is crucial to develop a coalition of stakeholders—such as colleagues, parents, and students—to advocate for change.

When it comes to working with school administration to develop and implement ABAR work, remember that there is no one go-to or one-size-fits-all approach. However, after speaking to a number of administrators and teachers from public, charter, and independent schools, certain strategies and approaches appeared to lead to successful conversations. Every administrator emphasized the importance of centering relationships, whether it was between a teacher and a principal, or the school and the families of the community.

The core of ABAR in any field is relationships and trust. For school administrators who are wary of their teachers facilitating lessons or conversations with young kids, transparency can often help. Consider approaching your principal or assistant principal from a place of co-construction and partnership by requesting support. Invite your administration into your classroom to observe a discussion or a read-aloud so they can see that kids are engaged, and that these topics should not be viewed as threatening.

For educators who seek to show their school leaders that ABAR work supports and challenges students within their curricular responsibilities, the template in Figure 5–2 is an example of how to proactively plan to defend your work. Check online for the blank template you can use.

# Taking Action in the Classroom: Teach Students to Talk About Their Learning

While this chapter has mainly focused on adult relationships, there are also classroom practices that can help support your case to your administrators. Give your students as many opportunities as possible to practice talking about their understanding. If your students are consistently able to use their vocabulary to clearly communicate about what

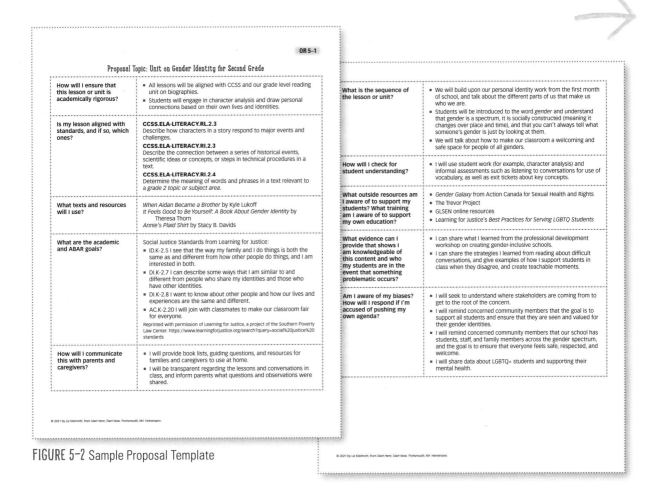

FIGURE 5–2 Sample Proposal Template

they are learning, it provides further evidence that this way of teaching is appropriate and accessible.

## Assign Classroom Ambassadors

Students in my classroom rotate different jobs every week, taking turns with responsibilities such as paper passer and crayon collector. One of the jobs is classroom ambassador. The classroom ambassador's job is to get up to greet any adult guest in our classroom if I am in the middle of teaching or working with another student. The classroom ambassador gives visitors a summary of the current lesson, a brief description of what we are studying in class, and answers any questions they might have. You might assign two or more students at a time to be ambassadors. As with any classroom job, you'll want to talk about the roles and expectations of classroom ambassadors. Create an anchor chart like the one in Figure 5–3 or support ambassadors with a quick summary of units, lessons, and goals. A summary example is in Figure 5–4. You'll find a blank template in the online resources. Provide support by reviewing the summary at a designated weekly time (my students rotated jobs weekly, so we went over job assignments and updates on Monday morning during our community circle) and having students practice explaining what your class is studying. Make sure you rotate the ambassador role so each student gets a turn.

My school and classroom had frequent visitors—prospective family tours, potential donors, district observations—all led by a member of our administration. Whenever we had visitors during an ABAR-focused lesson, my principal or assistant principal would hear students describe our lessons from their own perspectives. During the first month of school when I was teaching fourth grade, my principal came through my classroom with a group of prospective families while my students were engaged in an identity-based activity. When a few students were questioned about the lesson, I was proud to hear them share that they were using their identity maps to see what they had in common, and how they were different. My students' ability to speak for themselves to describe their learning demonstrated their fluency and comfort with the language of social identity markers, such as ethnicity, gender, and religion, further showing my administrators that this work is accessible and engaging for students. However, developing critical-thinking skills and having students practice explaining their thinking are crucial, and students should never be parroting the exact thoughts or opinions of their teacher.

**Roles and Expectations of Classroom Ambassadors**

- Greet visitors and introduce yourselves (name and pronouns)
- Summarize what we're studying (use our quick summary template)
- Ask visitors if they have any questions and answer them if you can
- Take visitors on a tour of our classroom
- Meet with teacher during job assignments time

FIGURE 5-3 Ambassador Anchor chart

| CLASSROOM AMBASSADOR WEEK OF _____ | OR 5–2 |
|---|---|
| **Quick Summary of What We're Studying** | |

| | |
|---|---|
| **What is our class' social justice focus?** | "This month our class is learning about activists and activism." |
| **How is it applied in our current math and science work?** | "In science class, we're learning about the water cycle, and we're also studying indigenous youth environmental activists." |
| **How is it applied in our current reading and writing work?** | "In reading and writing, we're studying books about the Civil Rights Movement, and learning to write persuasive letters." |
| **Classroom tour** | Take guests around the room and show and explain our published letters to local lawmakers, and our group science projects. |
| **Questions?** | Ask guests if they have any questions and try your best to answer. It's OK if you don't know! |

© 2021 by Liz Kleinroth, from *Start Here, Start Now.* Portsmouth, NH: Heinemann.

FIGURE 5–4 Sample Quick Summary of What We're Studying

# Creating a Sustainable Practice: Relationships Are at the Root of All ABAR Work

Relationships are at the root of all ABAR work, and that includes those between administrators and teachers. If you're noticing that teaching with an ABAR lens is having positive outcomes for your students, share these successes with both your principal and your students' families. I'll never forget a former student who often seemed uninterested in class and rarely volunteered to share out loud, but when we began a unit on immigration and xenophobia and what it means to be an accomplice and co-conspirator, there was a noticeable shift. He was eager to speak and verbalize his observations and wrote passionately about our book study. Later he told me that his parents were asylum seekers, and he was excited to have a space to talk about his family history. When it was time to look at student data, I was able to use his pre- and post-unit writing samples to demonstrate how his academic growth was positively affected by utilizing an ABAR topic.

At the end of the day, remember that teachers and administrators usually come from the same workspaces. Administrators want to improve their schools and better serve their teachers and students, but still need support and opportunities to learn from their staff. It's important that teachers see themselves as partners, not as adversaries, even if their principal doesn't agree just yet.

## How Do I Know If It's Working?

When I work with schools that are eager to start ABAR work, one of the first questions I ask is if the leadership knows how teachers, students, and families of marginalized identities are experiencing school, and how they feel. Not surprisingly, the answers usually involve speculation, but little else. To ensure that your school's ABAR work is meaningful rather than performative, make sure there are opportunities for families and caregivers to give their feedback and input for the vision of the school community. If you can utilize community experiences and input to demonstrate areas of growth and actionable steps and bring this information to your administration, you may find more success.

If you're in a position where your administration is open to ABAR teaching but says their plate is too full, consider how you can provide support by pointing them in the direction of resources and training. Some concrete steps you can take:

>> If you encounter ABAR professional development opportunities, forward them to your colleagues.

>> When your school begins planning the professional development calendar for the months ahead, ask to be a part of the conversation and come equipped with suggestions for sessions, as well as organizations or mentor texts to consult.

>> Ask if you and your colleagues can host a book club to focus on different ABAR topics and if your school will additionally compensate you for this work. Have each meeting focus on a different article or ask people to watch a documentary or TED Talk to allow for more participant flexibility.

>> Identify like-minded parents and caregivers to help organize workshops where staff and families can learn together.

In the case that you are a white teacher and your administrators identify as BIPOC, consider how you can act as an accomplice or co-conspirator. Perhaps your principal previously had a negative experience, or faced pushback from the superintendent, board members, or the parent and family community. How can you leverage your privilege to both support your administration and drive ABAR work forward?

## If All Else Fails

There is no blanket strategy for ABAR, so you must take your context into consideration. For educators who work in districts with strong unions, it will be easier to shift your teaching practices. For others who teach in places where if you upset your administration you can quickly be deemed ineffective and lose your job, you have to weigh your risks and determine what changes you can make within your control. For example, if your principal is adamant about following standards, carefully review them and your curriculum to determine if you can isolate standards and supplement additional materials to teach the particular topic. However, remember that ABAR is a lens, and your curriculum is just one aspect of your practice. Even if your administration is unsupportive of curricular integration, there is important self-work to do as a teacher, as well as intentionally creating the culture of your classroom.

## Don't Reinvent the Wheel

As the majority of this book focuses on identifying tools and strategies to work with young people, the following texts and articles are recommended to engage with other adults around potentially challenging conversations. I recognize that the existing power dynamic between a teacher and an administrator can pose an extra obstacle, so the more prepared you are, the better. These resources can help set you up for success and plan for your desired outcome, while preparing for pushback.

> » *Courageous Conversations About Race*, by Glenn E. Singleton

> » *The Five Dysfunctions of a Team*, by Patrick Lencioni

> » *Never Split the Difference*, by Christopher Voss with Tahl Raz

> » "What an Anti-Racist Principal Must Do," by Mark Anthony Gooden (*EdWeek*, October 13, 2020)

> » *A School Leader's Guide to Excellence,* by Carmen Fariña and Laura Kotch

> » "Avoiding Racial Equity Detours," by Paul Gorski (*Educational Leadership*, April 2019, Vol. 76, No. 7)

> » "Anti-Racist Work in Schools: Are You in It for the Long Haul?" by Liz Kleinrock (*Learning for Justice*, June 30, 2020)

# {6}

# What Does ABAR Look Like If All or Most of My Students Are White?

START HERE

**I'VE SPENT THE MAJORITY OF MY TEACHING CAREER**
working in diverse schools. Every fall, we begin the
year by having students participate in a number of activities and lessons
that develop their identities and discuss ways in which they're similar
and different. My students easily write, draw, and chatter about their
interests and hobbies, but every year without fail, some of my students
encounter a challenge. When it comes to talking about their ethnicity
and culture, my BIPOC students often easily identify and share about
their heritage. Many of my white students, however, approach me with
confusion: "I don't know what to write about for my culture. I don't think
I have one."

There's a story told by David Foster Wallace that captures this very
issue:

> There are these two young fish swimming along and they
> happen to meet an older fish swimming the other way, who
> nods at them and says, "Morning, boys. How's the water?"

> And the two young fish swim on for a bit, and then eventually one of them looks over at the other and goes, "What the hell is water?" (Wallace 2005, 3–4)

The United States is a racially and ethnically diverse country yet is still governed by white dominant culture (the idea that white people have shaped our society's norms, values, standards, and beliefs). If whiteness is the default, this means that people rarely have to define what it means to be white, or what white culture looks or sounds like. *Multiculturalism* often seems to encompass anything that falls outside of the dominant white, Eurocentric culture, so what does antibias and antiracist work look like if most or all of your students are white? How can teachers build agency for white students in ways that foster the positive identities that all children deserve? Ways that both acknowledge and push back against the dominance of whiteness?

The purpose of this chapter is not to make a blanket statement accusing predominantly white schools of not caring or not prioritizing initiatives around ABAR, but rather to explore how ABAR issues exist within white schools and need to be addressed in ways that fit the needs of the community. As I've traveled and talked to educators who work in majority-white schools, many have voiced questions about how to incorporate ABAR work in the classroom. Amy Melik (she/her), an English language learner coordinator and teacher in an affluent, majority-white district outside of Milwaukee, Wisconsin, described some common observations:

> In white communities, people don't see the need for this work. In affluent, majority-white schools that are performing highly and see high testing results, there might be a small percentage of students who aren't performing well, but if everyone else is, the schools do not perceive there to be a problem. I've found that there are a lot of silent cheerleaders who don't want to say anything because they're too afraid because they're worried about what others might say.

Some may even believe that it's not necessary to address diversity in white schools because kids must naturally absorb these ideas simply by living in a diverse country or watching shows or movies with diverse characters. However, it is not enough to hope that white children learn about differences through social osmosis or books and media about different people and cultures. If educators solely rely on diverse learning materials without modeling conversations and actively engaging with their students, we intellectualize the idea of diversity. Even meaningful books and realia can become a tourist curriculum (such as bringing in rice cakes for Lunar New Year or decorating sugar skulls for Dia de los Muertos). Students may be attracted to the items for the novel experiences but do not appreciate, understand, or respect different cultures and values. Exposure to different people, cultures, and histories is important, but without ongoing dialogue and critical thinking, it does not equate to creating inclusive practices, advocating for equity and justice, and loving and respecting people of color.

It can be challenging to talk and teach about race and diversity if your community isn't racially diverse. If all students and families identify as white, there may not be the same awareness of racially biased practices and beliefs that you might find in a diverse or predominantly Black or Brown community. However, many teachers express concern for the small number of students of color in their majority-white schools and recall times when their Black and Brown students were singled out in front of their peers during conversations about enslavement or the Civil Rights Movement. Friends and colleagues of color who once attended predominantly white schools have shared painful memories of feeling both tokenized and erased in the classroom and feeling unsupported and unsure of how to respond to peers' comments about their skin color and culture. I recall a colleague who recounted an experience as the only Black student in his elementary school class: "We were studying the Civil Rights Movement and I remember my teacher kept looking at me. I think she thought she was being subtle by sneaking glances, and maybe she didn't even notice, but I felt like she was putting me in the spotlight. Later when we were looking at a poster of the March on Washington, a kid in my class asked if I was related to the people in the photo and my teacher just ignored it." These students need to be seen in the classroom and school as experts in their own experiences without being positioned to speak on behalf of all people who look like them. (Additionally, it's important for white educators and school leaders to understand that not all teachers of color desire to be leaders in schoolwide initiatives, so check in before you assign them to be the head of the diversity committee.)

The fear that Melik described came up often in my conversations with teachers and staff in white schools. Many felt that advocating for ABAR work meant they had to walk on eggshells. They cited roadblocks they had encountered from others, such as "Diversity and antibias lessons exclude white children" and "I don't want white kids to feel ashamed of being white." There was also an ongoing theme of wanting to protect the innocence of white children, following the assumption that amplifying issues around ABAR would make them feel bad, and can't we just let kids be kids and enjoy their childhoods? To briefly address these concerns, I believe that all students, regardless of race, deserve to form positive self-identities. In the United States, however, it can be challenging to determine what it means to have a positive racial identity as a white person while separating a sense of racial superiority reinforced by white dominant culture. The desire to preserve the innocence of white children is a luxury that children of color do not experience. The white culture's perceived lack of innocence of Black children often leads to harsh disciplinary practices, as well as acts of violence such as the killing of Tamir Rice in 2014.

Diversity and antibias extend beyond the topic of race. Educator Emily Alt (she/her), who teaches at an entirely white school in northern Michigan, recalled a time when someone said to her, "It must be so boring to work at your school because all of your students are white." She responded, "Well, there's a lot of other types of diversity besides skin color. And it's not boring because I understand the urgency of this work. It's urgent wherever you are in whatever type of demographic you're working with. In rural education, educating white kids who have literally never interacted with another person of color and don't have the opportunities to meet people who are different, I can't imagine anything more urgent." She added, "However, something teachers have to unlearn is that work around race isn't for white kids. You can create significant change and empowerment really with any demographic of students that you're working with."

The Brazilian philosopher Paulo Freire (1970) wrote extensively about the relationship between the oppressed and the oppressor and reminds us that all-encompassing movements for liberation must include those from the dominant group. ABAR is not just for BIPOC and those who are marginalized—white folx must also be a part of this movement. I've often said that there is no one-size-fits-all when it comes to ABAR, but the work is still for everyone and includes everyone. I've worked with schools throughout the United States, and the needs of a school outside of Memphis are going to look different from those of an independent school in New England or a public school in East Los Angeles. A school may lack racial diversity but still possess diversity in terms of gender, sexual orientation, religion, language, socioeconomic status, disability, and neurodiversity. ABAR work has a place in every school, and even if you work in a racially homogenous environment, it's important for students to examine the similarities and differences between white people, social hierarchies, and power structures, and to develop empathy and understanding for why people should care for each other across differences.

## Setting Yourself Up for Success: Conversations Around Difference and Inclusion

Working with different schools from around the United States is one of the aspects that I love most about my work. It's fascinating to learn about diversity priorities and initiatives, as well as the challenges of different communities. However, it's disheartening to receive requests for staff training and family education as a result of a problematic student comment or action. In my experience, the two most common causes for these school requests have been white students wearing blackface, and issues concerning consent and harassment. When I work with these schools, the first question I ask is "No matter how subtle, what messages did your students receive that told them this type of behavior or language is acceptable?" Nearly every school has a diversity statement on their website, but preaching the value of diversity is not the same as teaching students to value and respect people who are different from themselves.

## Engage White Parents and Caregivers with a Weekly Wrap-Up

Many teachers who work in predominantly white schools cite additional issues such as conservative political and religious beliefs as barriers to ABAR work. "The challenge isn't so much working with white kids, as it is working with white parents," explained Melik. Often white parents will claim that they "don't see race" or express their desire to "protect their child's innocence." While I certainly understand a caregiver's wishes to shield their child from harm, pretending to ignore race or differences is not antiracist behavior. It's the equivalent of shoving your clothes under the bed instead of cleaning your room. It doesn't make the problem go away. In Chapter 1, where I share my identity map, I explain that I love and value the way I look and where I come from, but these aspects of my identity were rarely validated in school. As a person of color, my desire is for others to see me as I am and how I want to be seen without judging or treating me negatively. When you claim to not notice race, you're ignoring a part of me that I love about myself. Ignoring my race means that you see me only as you want to see me, rather than as I am. If white parents claim that talking about race compromises the innocence of their child, what message does that send to BIPOC children who are confronted with racism every day?

One of the most crucial steps to setting yourself up for success in this environment is to show and explain how the beauty of this work is that it benefits everyone. What kind of world do we want our children to inherit, and how are we committed to creating that world? What are the values we want to pass down to our children? If all people have biases and absorb messages from their environments, what can we do to ensure that white children do not hold or promote racist beliefs? What are we teaching white children if we act as though issues of antibias and antiracism don't concern them? When I work with white parents and educators, I often ask them to think about a time when they felt like an outsider. Nearly everyone has had an experience that left them feeling misunderstood, unheard, and unseen. The purpose of this work in schools is for our young people to recognize that people are multifaceted, everyone has an identity, and everyone's identity matters.

In the chapter that focuses on engaging parents and caregivers, I talk about the importance of transparency. For white parents who may be worried about how these conversations are held in class, it can ease some anxiety for them to have an idea of what's happening in the classroom. This can give them an access point for talking to their own children. An important part of my practice is to include a Weekly Wrap-Up email or letter to all families that gives an overview of what students learned that week, what we'll focus on in the week ahead, as well as any resources to support learning at home. Figure 6–1 is an example of one of my emails and Figure 6–2 shows a template you can use.

## 4th Grade Weekly Wrap-Up
### VOL. 14

Dear parents and families,

Thank you to everyone who participated in family–teacher conferences! It was wonderful to have time to speak with you all and discuss your students' progress in school!

### No homework over winter break!
*(But practicing times tables and reading never hurts!)*

**Day of Action!**

Please join us on our next Day of Action to recruit new students and families to the community. The purpose of these days is to engage staff and families around a collective action to drive enrollment at our schools.

**Table Talk**

Ask your kiddo about "The Bear That Wasn't," and how the opinions of others impact our own identities.

**Resource of the Week**

Learn about how the end of Net Neutrality could impact our classrooms
Next Dates: January 6th, February 3rd (likely 12-3pm)

Sign up here!

**This week . . .**

In SEL, students delved further into their identities and read stories about how our identities can be influenced by the opinions of others. We also explored "The Danger of a Single Story," and learned about how a single narrative can lead to biases about groups of people.

In Writer's Workshop, students reviewed paragraph structures such as topic sentence, supporting sentences, and concluding sentences.

In Reader's Workshop, students completed their research projects and presented them to the class!

In math, students wrapped up part 1 of our fraction unit by learning about equivalent fractions, and adding fractions with unlike denominators.

**Coming soon . . .**

December 18th–January 2nd
Winter Vacation

First day back is January 3rd!
This is a FULL DAY SCHEDULE!!! Dismissal at 3:15!

January 15th
No school in honor of Dr. Martin Luther King Jr. Day

Have a great vacation!

**Ms. Liz & The 4th Grade Team**
NO HOMEWORK OVER BREAK!!!

*Ask your kiddo about "The Bear That Wasn't," and how the opinions of others impact our own identities.*

**Resource of the Week:**
Learn about how the end of Net Neutrality could impact our classrooms

FIGURE 6–1 (*above*) Weekly Wrap-Up Email Example

FIGURE 6–2 (*right*) Weekly Wrap-Up Planning Template

OR 6–1

### Weekly Wrap-Up Planning Template

| | |
|---|---|
| What did your class learn this week in each subject? | |
| What did your class do as a community this week? | |
| What questions can caregivers ask their child at home to discuss their learning and understanding? | |
| What resource(s) can caregivers use to educate themselves? | |
| What community events and upcoming dates do families need to know about? | |

© 2021 by Liz Kleinroth, from *Start Here, Start Now*. Portsmouth, NH: Heinemann.

## Center the Voices of BIPOC from an Asset-Based Perspective

One of the most frequent challenges I notice when working in predominantly white schools is the nuance of ABAR work. Each situation may require a different action. For example, BIPOC voices and experiences must be centered in ABAR work, but schools cannot expect staff, students, and families of color to do the emotional labor or display their trauma for others' learning. Most of the educators I encounter who work in white schools understand the importance of teaching diverse perspectives in history, but they worry about representing the experiences of people of color when there aren't any in the room. Educator Bria Wright (she/her) of Raleigh, North Carolina, teaches in a majority-white school and gave a reminder that even educators of color in white schools have to be mindful of the voices they amplify. "The other day, I was looking through my own classroom library and doing an inventory about my books on American enslavement," she shared. "I pulled out my books and I put the ones to the side that weren't by Black authors. To me, this isn't really a white woman or man's story to tell. Auditing our books and authors to see if they're representing those who share their background is an easy way to avoid centering whiteness when teaching predominantly white students."

I also caution teachers of white students to consider how and when they teach about people of color. If white children who grow up in racially homogenous communities learn about Black and Brown people and history only through the lens of enslavement and oppression, how might this trajectory impact how they interact with people of color? Dr. Beverly Daniel Tatum, author of *Why Are All the Black Kids Sitting Together in the Cafeteria?* (2017), reminds us that representation alone is not enough; we have to think about *how* marginalized peoples are portrayed. As an East Asian American student, the only times I saw myself in the curriculum were when learning briefly about the Chinese Exclusion Act and the internment of Japanese Americans during WWII. How would my identity be different now if my classmates and I had learned about the lives and activism of Grace Lee Boggs, Yuri Kochiyama, or Mabei Ping-Hua Lee? If the only representation of marginalized people in your classroom focuses on injustices they have experienced, it further perpetuates feelings of pity, white saviorism, and paternalism.

# Taking Action in the Classroom: Embrace the Beauty and Messiness of Diversity

One of the most annoying representations of diversity is the image of people from different backgrounds standing in a circle holding hands. Diversity and multiculturalism are far too often presented as ideals and, while diversity is beautiful, we need to be realistic about the messiness that comes with being around people who are different.

## Chart the Benefits and Challenges of Diversity

During one of our first classes, my students and I make a list of all the ways in which people are similar and different. The kids come up with identity markers such as age, gender, language spoken at home, and religion, and also list characteristics like height, favorite food, number of siblings, and what sports people play. We follow up this conversation by making a chart like the one in Figure 6–3. We talk about the challenges and benefits of diversity—how differences enhance our understanding of the world, but also how diversity challenges us through power-based hierarchies, disagreements that may arise, and how hard it can be to make sure everyone has a place at the table.

FIGURE 6–3 Benefits and Challenges of Diversity chart

## Make Venn Diagrams in Pairs Using Identity Maps

Even within racially homogenous classrooms, students need to explore both seen and unseen differences in their environment. Start with identity maps. Use the template in Online Resource 1–4 from Chapter 1. After students create individual identity maps, like the one in Figure 6–4 created by a fourth-grade white student, pair them together to create Venn diagrams that show the ways in which they are similar and different. Earlier in this chapter I mentioned working with white students who are unsure of their culture and ethnicity. Using identity maps as teaching tools is an effective way to show students that culture is multifaceted. We may share certain cultural aspects with others, while other characteristics may be unique to us or to another particular group. For older students, this is an opportunity to discuss the idea of *dominant culture*, for some students may take for granted that aspects of their identities, such as being cisgender or Christian, are part of the dominant norm in our society.

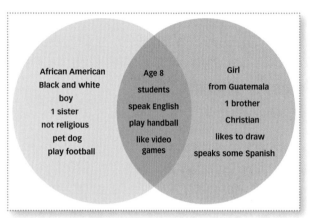

African American
Black and white
boy
1 sister
not religious
pet dog
play football

Age 8
students
speak English
play handball
like video
games

Girl
from Guatemala
1 brother
Christian
likes to draw
speaks some Spanish

FIGURE 6–4 Students' Venn Diagram

What do we THINK we
know about Africa?

Grasslands   Deserts   The   Kenya
sand   Lion King
Slavery   Tropical
Not   Most
No cities   many   Small   People are poor
or cars   people   towns
Hot
Safaris   Poor   Dry
parts
People   Animals   Lions +
of Color   everywhere   giraffes
Some
modern   "Heart   Tribes
parts   of the Earth"
Pyramids   Dangerous   Crops

FIGURE 6–5 What Do We Think We Know
About Africa? chart

## Create What Do We Think We Know? Charts

At the beginning of every year, before we study enslavement and the Civil Rights Movement, I ask my students to list all of the things they *think* they know about the African continent. In the chart in Figure 6–5, you can see that my students take on a deficit lens and list things like "Not many people," "Most people are poor," and an abundance of safari animals. After we're finished with the list, I ask my students if they've ever been to any country in Africa. Year after year, not one hand is raised. This leads us to the important question: If you haven't been to any African country, where did these ideas come from? If students become embarrassed when they realize they've listed stereotypes, I remind them that every single person has biases, and there's power in naming our biases. When biases are visible, we're better able to critique our own thinking and change our behavior. After all, it's difficult to fix problems that we're unaware of.

After this activity, my class watches Chimamanda Ngozi Adichie's TED Talk, "The Danger of a Single Story" (2009). In this talk, she discusses the ways in which our views of other people are often shaped by single stories that grow to represent and stereotype entire communities. For example, her white, American college roommate was surprised to learn that Adichie spoke English and could use a stove, because her

views about people from Africa were shaped by a single story of poverty and disaster. After my students watch her talk and read the transcript, we discuss how stereotypical thinking is constructed, and where we get our messages. To flip our perspective, we then imagine what people outside of the United States might think about us. What kinds of single stories might people in other countries be hearing and reading that inform their ideas about who we are? If they are solely relying on a single story of the United States, what parts would they be missing? Figure 6–6 shows an example of a chart we made. I find this to be an impactful

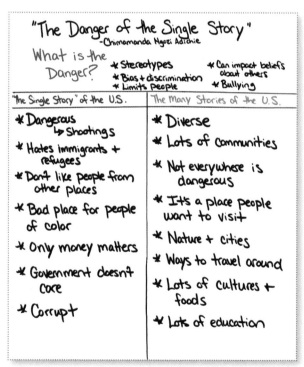

FIGURE 6–6 Danger of a Single Story chart

exercise not only for students, but also for educators when considering how to teach from a multicultural lens. If a limited number of diverse perspectives are offered, what single stories might students be drawing from when forming their ideas about different people?

## Help Students Unpack White Identity

Earlier in this chapter, I touched briefly on the importance of avoiding tokenization when it comes to teaching about identities and histories that are not reflected in your student body. Assembling a classroom library of diverse books and incorporating lessons about different cultures, backgrounds, and beliefs are great starting points for diversifying your curriculum, but how these conversations are framed is just as important. A fifth-grade teacher in Michigan recalled a lesson taught by a white colleague to a class of white students where they participated in a slave ship reenactment. (I want to emphasize for teachers that racialized reenactments or reenactments based on trauma, whether about enslavement, Indigenous tribes, the Holocaust, or any other group of people, is never acceptable or respectful.) While some members of the community were appalled, the teacher insisted that she had succeeded in teaching about enslavement in a way that was interactive for her students. Lessons should never reinforce stereotypes, dehumanize, or assume that white students learn to understand or respect the experiences of people of color by taking on the role of a character.

With older students, Emily Alt suggests shifting your teaching lens to help white students examine their books and lessons from a different perspective. While Alt previously taught in diverse schools, and schools with majority students of color, she reflected on the differences in how she approaches conversations in her entirely white class. She regards racial justice work with white students as crucial for their own development and understanding of their racialized identity, giving the example of what it looks like to teach the book *To Kill a Mockingbird* by Harper Lee (1960) to a class of all white students. Alt shared, "When you teach this book to students of color, they recognize the nuances of the white savior complex. They can see Atticus for the complex character that he is, and that he's not just this great lawyer who just wanted to do something nice for a Black man. Whereas when my white students read that novel, they love Atticus. They think he's so open to everything and they don't see a lot of the different perspectives in play, and how it might portray communities of color needing a white man to come in and save them."

While people of color are confronted with their racialized identities every day, rarely are white children and adults required to do the same. Far too often, this idea is confused with forcing white children to feel guilt or shame, and I find that forcing people to feel shame is both unproductive and ineffective to the greater goal of achieving social justice. Helping white students develop an awareness of being white encourages them to explore their own identities, reflect on how they view themselves and others in their communities, and empower them to create change in favor of racial equity and inclusion. Racial literacy doesn't mean being able to talk only about the races of other people; it also means recognizing how your own race impacts your perspective and lived experience.

Last year, I taught a weekly class that happened to be comprised of white students, most of whom came from financially privileged backgrounds. In a city as diverse as Los Angeles, I had a unique opportunity to dive into questions and topics around whiteness and create an affinity space to talk specifically about racial identity. The chart in Figure 6–7, Unpacking White Identity, was co-created with students. I asked them to simply answer the questions written on the poster. My students were in third, fourth, and fifth grades, and while I was not surprised to hear that they didn't think much about their race on a daily basis, I found it fascinating that these children were aware of the discomfort felt by white adults, and could articulate why some white adults struggle with talking about race. Every child

**FIGURE 6–7** Unpacking White Identity chart

was aware of the dominance of whiteness in history and how people of color have been oppressed because of their race. Ultimately, I found that these kids were able to acknowledge racism in the United States' history, and to understand that being white has been and still remains advantageous. I wanted to make sure my lessons focused on identity and being proactive, so we talked about the fact that there is nothing shameful about being white, and that they are not expected to atone or fix what has happened in the past. If you recognize that you live in a world where you benefit from the color of your skin, what matters is what you do with that knowledge moving forward.

## Examine Privilege

Educators of white students often express their desire to talk about white privilege in their communities. This term tends to elicit strong emotional reactions in certain white people, especially those who have struggled financially or believe that the United States is an equitable meritocracy that will reward all who pull themselves up by their bootstraps. When I first taught lessons about privilege, I wanted my students to understand that privilege comes in many forms, and that certain identity markers or characteristics benefit us and challenge us in different ways. We talked about financial privilege, privilege around ability and disability, body type, gender, and religion, as seen in Figure 6–8. Many of my Christian students were struck when they were asked to imagine a holiday season without public places decked out in red and green or their traditional songs played in stores, and them needing to take unexcused absence days from school to celebrate the holiday with their family. Since none of my students are deaf, it never occurred to them that it's a privilege to be able to watch a movie at any time at any theater, rather than only being able to attend screenings with closed captions.

My opinions and language around *privilege* have shifted since the first time I taught these lessons. At first, the objective was to have students examine ways they could use their privilege to help others, and now we discuss how it is necessary to give up or *spend* their privilege to contribute to the liberation of the oppressed. To start this dialogue, when I talk about the concept of privilege with my students, we critically examine the ways in which they navigate the world with ease because certain systems have been designed for them to thrive. By recognizing how they possess privileges that others don't have, we're able to discuss how to make our communities more inclusive for all people. We create a chart like the one in Figure 6–8.

When it comes to introducing examples of white people who used their privileges to advocate for people of color, be mindful of perpetuating the savior narrative. (Think of the movie *Freedom Writers*, where a white female teacher is portrayed as single-handedly turning around the lives of her Black and Brown inner-city students.) One individual whom I amplify in my class is Joan Trumpauer Mulholland, a white female civil rights activist who participated in the Freedom Rides. Her lifework is an example of a white antiracist person who worked with and alongside the Black community and made the choice to use her voice and privilege to create positive change in the world. Another person my class studies is Irena Sendler, a Polish nurse and social worker who risked her

FIGURE 6–8 Spending Your Privilege chart

| How Can You Spend Your Privilege? | |
| --- | --- |
| Type of privilege | How you can spend it |
| Financial | ■ Redistribute your money by giving to under-resourced communities and organizations. |
| Racial | ■ If you are white or a non-Black person of color, interrupt when you hear anti-Black bias and racism, even if it makes people uncomfortable. |
| Religious | ■ Speak up when you hear biases against religious minorities.<br>■ Remind others that "The Holidays" in December do not reflect everyone's religious or cultural beliefs and practices. |
| Gender | ■ Introduce yourself with your pronouns, especially if you are cisgender.<br>■ Respect people's gender identity.<br>■ Speak up against gender stereotypes. |
| Ableness | ■ Correct people who use ableist language like *crazy* or *lame*.<br>■ Advocate for people with disabilities in your community. |

life to smuggle supplies into the Warsaw Ghetto during the Holocaust. Despite being arrested and tortured by the Nazi police, she refused to give up any information and assisted over twenty-five hundred Jewish children to escape certain death.

# Creating a Sustainable Practice: The Importance of White People in ABAR Work

While advocating for social justice in predominantly white schools can be difficult for a myriad of reasons, it is crucial to consider how students may interpret the silence of adults on matters of identity, bias, and race. In many cases, this silence may speak louder than any book or lesson. If white children are not encouraged to think critically about antiracism and racial justice, they will not understand that they are also stakeholders in creating a more inclusive world. Diversity work will be viewed as a domain for other groups of people whose day-to-day lives are more directly impacted by bias and discrimination. When I discussed white identity with my recent class, it was important for these students to explicitly state why their participation matters. Their responses are charted in Figure 6–9. They agreed that white people have a responsibility to educate themselves about the lived experiences of people of different races, and that they themselves should have the opportunity to learn about themselves. One student commented

> **Why** should white people learn about race? (including their own)
>
> * We need to know about the past in order to change it
>
> * Learning about race will change our perspective
>   ↳ How we act, our decisions
>
> * So we can stop being racist
>
> * We can learn to treat people respectfully
>   ↳ Change our behavior

FIGURE 6–9 Why Should White People Learn About Race? chart

that learning about race could change people's perspectives, and that shifting our perspective can impact the way we think and act for the better. Another child declared, "It's going to be impossible for people to stop being racist if they don't even know when they're doing it!"

## How Do I Know If It's Working?

In ABAR workshops I facilitate that focus on racialized identity, I'll often ask participants when they first became aware of their race. For almost every BIPOC in attendance, they can usually pinpoint a moment in early childhood or adolescence. For white attendees, their racialized identity awareness did not come until much later. While discomfort is a natural and necessary part of ABAR work, I'm not advocating to make white students intentionally feel uncomfortable. It's important to create a space for all students to develop awareness of their identities and be comfortable talking about who they are. Figure 6–10 shows a chart of my white students' reflections about their racialized identity, and nearly all of them gave examples of times when they noticed white adults in their lives display discomfort when race and racism were discussed. During this conversation, I listened closely for signs of students internalizing guilt or shame and was proud to hear the children talk about the responsibility of white people to educate each other about racism, and what it means to be an aspiring antiracist white person.

FIGURE 6–10 Awareness of Being White chart

To track student understanding, I often use the sentence frame, "I used to think . . . but now I know . . ." as an opportunity for students to reflect on their learning and unlearning. You can see an example of one student's response in Figure 6–11. This sentence frame can be used to have students think about what they're learning about their own identities, as well as social justice issues and topics. It can provide concrete evidence to support student discussion and identify lingering biases.

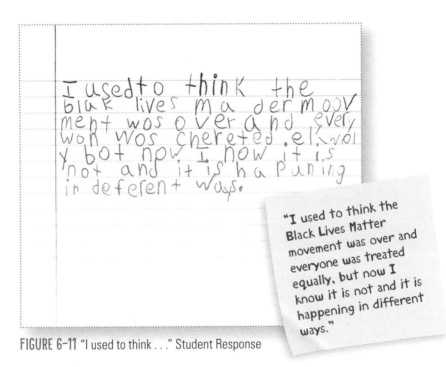

I used to think the blak lives ma der moov ment wos over and every won wos chereted .el wol y bot now I now it is not and it is ha puning in deferent ways.

"I used to think the Black Lives Matter movement was over and everyone was treated equally, but now I know it is not and it is happening in different ways."

FIGURE 6–11 "I used to think . . ." Student Response

## Don't Reinvent the Wheel

Sustaining social justice work in white schools requires teachers to keep in mind that student identities and the concept of diversity are multifaceted. While race is a pivotal identity marker for those living in the United States, even white homogenous schools are diverse in many ways. Students need to understand that aspects of people's identities are both visible and invisible and may be unsupported when it comes to understanding and respecting differences around gender, sexuality, religion, income, or disability. How can these diverse identities also be incorporated into existing lessons and units of study in a way that does not *other* those who do not belong to the dominant culture? In Figure 6–12, you'll see an example of how I incorporated diverse texts into a reading unit that focused on fairy and folk tales. The original curriculum instructed that students explore multiple versions of the *Cinderella* story, which is Eurocentric, and many of the recommended diverse texts, such as *The Rough-Face Girl* by Rafe Martin (1998) and *The Korean Cinderella* by Shirley Climo (1993), are penned by white authors.

Again, I want to emphasize the pitfalls of introducing diverse histories and narratives only in specific moments throughout the school year. This is not to say that topics like Black history should not be celebrated in February, but rather that they belong in the curriculum year-round. Additionally, just because no one in the immediate community reflects a certain culture or identity does not mean these topics should be ignored. Many people are familiar with Dr. Rudine Sims Bishop's work about how texts can serve as "mirrors, windows, and sliding glass doors" (1990, x), meaning that students might see themselves represented or gain new perspectives through different stories and lessons. In order to execute this well, the creators of diverse classroom resources should reflect the identities and stories they teach. Over the past few years I've conducted audits of my classroom library and lesson-planning resources and have found that a number of picture books that tell the stories of marginalized people were written by white authors. When people ask if I'm being overly sensitive about the sources of these stories, I respond by asking, "Is it important for you to tell your own story? How would you feel about someone who doesn't share your background profiting and receiving

FIGURE 6–12 Diverse Fairy and Folk Tales with Places of Origin

| Title | Origin |
|---|---|
| *Celtic Tales* by Kate Forrester | Ireland, Scotland, Brittany, and Wales |
| *Korean Children's Favorite Stories* by Kim So-Un | Korea |
| *Mazel and Shlimazel* by Isaac Bashevis Singer | Jewish Poland |
| *Lon Po Po* by Ed Young | China |
| *Ananse and the Lizard* by Pat Cummings | West Africa |
| *The Lizard and the Sun* by Alma Flor Ada | Aztec |

recognition for telling your story?" The chart in Figure 6–13 offers one example of how educators can analyze different resources to ensure that authors and resources reflect diverse backgrounds. You'll find a blank template for this form in the online resources.

Creating pathways for long-term sustainability for antibias and antiracist work can be exhausting in any school, and potentially even more challenging if the lack of surface-level diversity leads community members to believe that it shouldn't be prioritized or doesn't require space. It's not about teaching children what to think, it's about providing them with opportunities to practice *how* to think and expand their perspectives beyond their immediate community. At the end of the day, this work is for everyone. It benefits every student.

OR 6–2

### Checking Sources Planning Template

| Topic | Resource | Creator(s) | Type of Resource | Publication Year | Resources (Primary vs. Secondary?) |
|---|---|---|---|---|---|
| Indigenous people | Illuminatives.org | Founded by Crystal Echo Hawk, created and led by Native people | Curriculum, teaching guides | 2018 | Mix of primary and secondary |
| Gender identity and expression | *When Aidan Became a Brother* | Written by Kyle Lukoff, a transgender librarian and educator<br><br>Illustrated by Kaylani Juanita, a Black female artist | Picture book | 2019 | Secondary (narrative fiction) |
| Enslavement in the United States | Learning with Justice's *Teaching Hard History* (podcast and publication) | Led by Dr. Hasan Jeffries, professor of African American history at Ohio State University. Multiple contributors of diverse backgrounds (historians, K–12 educators, college professors). | Curriculum, lesson plans, reading texts | 2018 | Mix of primary and secondary sources |

FIGURE 6–13 Sample Checking Sources Planning Template

# { 7 }

# What Does Developmentally Appropriate ABAR Look Like for Younger Students?

**WHAT IS THE FIRST THING THAT COMES TO MIND** when you think of elementary school? A quick image search would result in pictures that feature smiling children sitting in circles, drawing with crayons, or playing with those huge rainbow parachutes. Many of these pictures represent the idealization of childhood and reflect an inherent sense of innocence that we believe all children possess. From the perspective of many educators and family members, childhood is a time for kids to be carefree and unburdened by the social and political issues that permeate our communities. If young children seem content playing games and reading books about talking animals, is it even appropriate to introduce topics like race and gender and introduce them to concerns they don't even know exist?

Despite our desire to create a world for our children that is free from prejudice and discrimination, it is often the naivety and discomfort of adults that prevent young students from learning about the world. Research studies have found that at birth, babies look equally at faces of all races, but at three months, babies look more at the faces that resemble the race of their parents and caregivers (Kelly et al. 2005). Additionally, children as young as two and three years old use race to choose their playmates (Katz and Kofkin 1997), and by kindergarten, children show many of the same racial attitudes held by adults in our culture (Kinzler 2016). However, a study by Bronson and Merryman (2009) concluded that if explicit conversations about interracial friendships are held with children between the ages of five and seven, their racial attitudes can be improved in as little as a week. With this knowledge and awareness, it is crucial that young children have the opportunity to learn about what makes them similar and different to others, share their experiences and observations, and ask questions.

Children might not be sitting around discussing critical race theory or intersectional feminism, but that doesn't mean that their conversations and interactions aren't touching on those exact subjects in ways that align with their maturity and social awareness. In my years teaching elementary school, I've overheard students make the following comments to each other:

> **"You can't be Captain America. He's white."**

> **"Girls aren't as good at four square as boys are."**

> **"This table is only for girls who love BTS."**

Comments like these are prevalent in elementary school, and even though children may not always be able to articulate where these statements come from, they still reflect their understandings about identity, power, and exclusion. Most commonly, I recall any statement made about a person's race being followed by a chorus of "Ohhhh that's racist!" when the original comment was simply an indication of the person's identity. Recently, I asked a group of middle schoolers to raise their hand if their first formal conversation about race was focused on enslavement or the Civil Rights Movements. Nearly every student raised their hand. We then began to discuss the implications of our first conversations about race happening years after children begin to notice race, and what it meant for the discussions to be focused solely on oppression and injustice. If the topic of race is immediately linked to some of the worst horror stories in history, an atmosphere of fear and anxiety arises whenever race comes up in conversation. If we can see from the research that people begin to notice different identity markers as early as infancy, what happens if biases and assumptions go unnoticed and unaddressed throughout childhood?

Teaching kids about diversity and antiracism is not about teaching them *what* to think. It's about giving students tools, strategies, and opportunities to practice *how* to think. Consider how we teach students to read. We build a foundation of literacy by breaking down words into letters and sounds. We encourage our students to develop fluency by reading every day. We encourage them to read aloud with a partner, with a group, and alone. We ask them comprehension questions to check for understanding. We gauge what our students are grasping, and how they can apply what they know to the world around them. I believe that antibias and antiracism in education should be approached in the same way. We can introduce foundational vocabulary and understanding around these topics and encourage students to speak, share, and practice what they learn with others.

For many educators, their own experiences and discomfort are the reasons why they avoid facilitating conversations around race with young students. Children can be blunt, their ideas and opinions flow out of them like water, and they sometimes speak in sweeping generalizations without knowing social and historical context for their comments. However, these fears are also why early childhood and elementary school teachers should take advantage of this developmental period. Early childhood and antibias researcher Louise Derman-Sparks explains, "Children live in a world that sends multiple, stereotype-laden messages about their comparative value, their right to be visible, and how they are expected to behave based on their economic class, ethnicity, gender, abilities, racial identity, and religion. These overt and covert messages affect their own sense of self-worth and how they think about people who are different" (Derman-Sparks and Edwards 2020, 124). Consider all the things that young people are exposed to. They see, hear, and take in everything that adults do, except they're given far less context and information because adults too often make the assumption that children don't understand, can't understand, or shouldn't understand. When we act like young learners can't or don't understand what's going on in our world, we do them a disservice. For example, if children are walking around with misinformation about different groups of people, that misinformation influences their biases and beliefs about others. Those biases influence how they may or may not interact with others throughout their lives.

Thinking back to the uncomfortable moment with my students when I heard them making comments that could be interpreted as racist, sexist, or homophobic, I knew that how I chose to respond in those moments could have had lifelong implications for these children and the other students in my class. If teachers ignore these comments, our students might infer that these types of comments are acceptable. If we harshly reprimand our students and shame them in front of their peers, the feeling of embarrassment associated with their early conversations around differences might prevent them from engaging in the future. To avoid both of these undesirable scenarios, we can set ourselves up for success directly countering the stereotypes we see perpetuated in our classrooms and on the playground.

# Setting Yourself Up for Success: Identify Foundational Building Blocks

There are significant implications when teachers do not engage their students around issues of race and multiple perspectives in history. For example, a 2018 study by the Southern Poverty Law Center's Learning for Justice found that only 8 percent of high school seniors could name enslavement as the central cause of the Civil War. Other studies have recently shown similar gaps in our historical knowledge, which impacts the treatment of marginalized people. If we proactively address the foundational concepts around race and justice, we might be able to prevent hate crimes in the future and build bridges across differences. While this can feel overwhelming, just remember that all of these conversations start somewhere.

## Backward Planning That's Developmentally Appropriate

When it comes to social justice work with young children, I prefer to backward plan and think about what understandings need to be in place before engaging with complex topics. Figure 7–1 shows how I've

OR 7–1

## Sample Topics and What Young Learners Need to Understand First

| The Big Topic | What Do My Students Need to Understand First? |
|---|---|
| Incarceration | How is a punishment different from a consequence? What does it mean for something to be fair or equal? |
| Racism | Where does skin color come from? What does it mean to have power? |
| Migrant detention centers | What is an immigrant? Why do people leave their homes? Who is a citizen? How do people become citizens? |
| LGBTQ+ rights and representation | What is gender identity? What is gender expression? How are families similar and different? |
| Sexual harassment | Consent, respecting physical boundaries, physical safety |

FIGURE 7–1 Sample Topics and What Young Learners Need to Understand First

laid out a few pathways for building scopes and sequences for teaching about different social issues. Use the blank template in the online resources to identify pathways for your scopes and sequences. With elementary-age children, it can be particularly intimidating to figure out what's developmentally appropriate to talk about. What does antibias and antiracist work even look like with young kids?

For example, kindergarteners are most likely not ready to start talking about mass incarceration. But a kindergartener can understand the concepts of what is *fair* (everyone getting what they need) versus what is *equal* (everyone getting the same thing), what is a *punishment*, and how a punishment is different from a *consequence*. These are all foundational concepts that everyone needs to understand in order to comprehend, later on, the issues surrounding incarceration in the United States. Perhaps those students are too young to tackle racism, but they need to start with understanding the components that make up our identities, how people are similar and different, and what it means to have power when others do not.

With your grade team or trusted colleagues, take some time to brainstorm big topics and what your students need to understand first. Think about current events and the issues that impact your community or that your students have seen in the media, such as anti-Blackness, Black Lives Matter and police bias, sexual harassment, political elections, and anti-immigration sentiment.

## Taking Action in the Classroom: Gather Background Knowledge and Generate Questions

Conversations about ABAR have their own language, and young students need to become literate in that language so they can actually talk about issues that are so often taboo but so core to the human experience. Schools are often the only places where children can feel free to make mistakes and learn from them, and unfortunately not all children feel that security. When educators or parents ask me, "How do you make topics like race or gender accessible and appropriate for young learners?" I always answer, "Start by asking these children what they already know, and what questions they have." To assume that students are too young, too naive, or too indifferent to notice insults their intelligence. How can we hope to prepare them to become active, engaged citizens in our world if we don't invite them to talk about the very world they're living in?

Language is a crucial component of cultivating a classroom that is focused on ABAR, equity, and inclusion. While labeling can be problematic when it comes to stereotyping and making generalizations, naming issues can also hold great power because children can learn how to describe different experiences and learn that they are not alone. For example, as a transracial adoptee, I wish that someone had taught me what *imposter syndrome* meant when I was a child and constantly felt like I wasn't "Asian enough," because I would have felt less isolated knowing that others felt the same way, and that my identity as an adopted Korean American is part of the Asian diaspora.

## ABAR Word Wall

One of the first steps I take when setting up a lesson focused on a social justice issue is to deliberately introduce vocabulary and definitions that will support my students' understanding. In addition to math and language arts word walls, I also create an ABAR word wall like the one in Figure 7–2. My students and I move slowly, focusing on only one or two new words per lesson. Whenever we begin, I display the word and first ask my class if anyone is familiar with it and what it means. Often the words are new to them; but on occasion, when a student knows a word, it's empowering when they can teach their peers what they know.

Sometimes it helps to give them a scenario that helps them define a word. For example, "We know that in math, the equal sign means *the same as*. If a group of people are treated *equally*, what does that tell us about how they're treated?" In other instances, you might break down recognizable parts of words: "Let's look at the word *dehumanize*. What root word do you know within the larger word? We also learned about prefixes and suffixes, so what do *de-* and *-ize* do to the meaning of the word?"

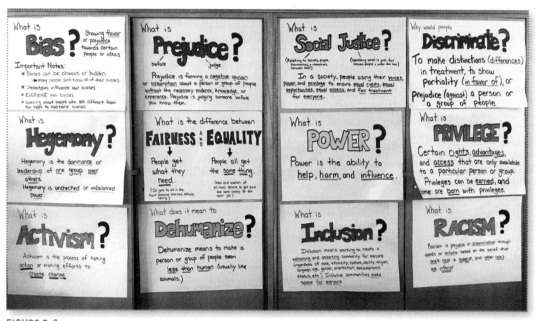

FIGURE 7-2 ABAR Word Wall

The word wall should be a living document in your classroom. The words should be edited when you learn new information or connect to new examples. This was especially important for my students who were emerging bilinguals or students with disabilities. They benefited from visual references. My students were never expected to memorize these words; rather they were tools they could access and use whenever they needed.

## Revisit KWL Charts

Have you ever asked a child what they're curious about? Their responses could fill volumes. Whenever we start a new unit in my class, we create a KWL chart ("What do we KNOW? What do we WANT to know? What have we LEARNED?") and start with two very simple questions: "What do you know about this topic already?" and "What questions do you have?" By asking these questions, I can get a sense of their experiences and background knowledge.

Sometimes I worry about keeping my beliefs in check. In order to prevent myself from preaching from the pulpit, I want my students' inquiries to constantly guide our learning and discussion. Before we read a biography of Harriet Tubman, my third-grade class and I created the KWL chart in Figure 7–3. I was concerned that eight- and nine-year-olds

The Legacy of Enslavement

| KNOW | WANT TO KNOW | LEARNED |
|---|---|---|
| * Most enslaved people were in the South | * How were Africans enslaved? | |
| * Black people were enslaved by white people | * Were enslaved people freed or released? | |
| * Enslaved people died trying to escape | * How many white people helped w/ the Underground Railroad? | |
| * Enslaved Africans were taken by boats | * Was there such thing as a "nice" enslaver? | |
| * Enslaved people were auctioned + dehumanized | * Which states had enslaved people? | |
| * Enslaved people did not have good food | * Why was slavery more popular in the South? | |
| * Enslaved people kept trying to escape | * Were these enslaved people on the west coast? | |
| * Frederick Douglass + Harriet Tubman | | |

FIGURE 7–3 Third-Grade KWL chart Before Beginning Lessons on Enslavement in the United States

did not have enough background knowledge about enslavement in the United States and would have a difficult time understanding the significance of Harriet Tubman's life without understanding the historical context in which she lived. Collecting my students' prior knowledge was helpful in gauging what they knew of the historical context and revealing gaps in their understanding. Some of my students had read books about Harriet Tubman's life at home. A few had learned a song about enslaved people following the North Star to freedom during Black History Month the prior year. From our KWL chart, I also saw that some students in my class focused on the resilience of enslaved people and the choices made by enslavers. They understood that Black people had resisted enslavement and never stopped fighting for their freedom. My students' questions revealed curiosity about the morality of white people during this time. My observations from this KWL chart reminded me that the biggest impact I could make on my students would be to focus on specific narratives and humanize both Black and white people. In the big picture, I wanted my students to understand that whole groups of people don't wake up one day and decide to oppress another group of people, but rather individuals make choices based on biases and prejudice that over time impact the beliefs and actions of entire communities.

## Consider What Kids Already Know About Social Justice from Shared Experiences

### BRAINSTORM QUESTIONS

A few years ago, I taught a weekly after-school class to third, fourth, and fifth graders, solely focused on social justice issues. At our first class I asked students to list questions around social justice, equity, and inclusion. Figure 7–4 shows what they came up with. The chart is simply a list of topics they had heard about. When I asked them how they had heard about these issues, they cited situations like listening in on their parents talking with each other, catching a glimpse of a newspaper headline, or reading a headline or article on social media.

Social Justice Inquiry
* What is the Holocaust?
    + What sparked it?
* Can we learn about the harder parts
  of history in order to fix it?
* What are the social justice issues
    of today?    * What are all the injustices?
* Uncover truths in our history
* What can we do to stop injustice?
    * Small acts + microaggressions
* What can we do to learn more?
* How did racism start?
* Who are not famous people who helped?
* Why did Europeans want to wipe out
    Indigenous peoples?

FIGURE 7-4 Questions About Social Justice, Equity, and Inclusion

## FAIR VS. EQUAL

One of the first conversations I have with my students is about the difference between something being *equitable* or *fair*, and something being *equal*. Most children have an understanding of these concepts and can identify situations when they felt they were treated fairly or unfairly. By beginning here, all students are able to engage and show that they do have prior knowledge and experience with these ideas. Additionally, this can be an opportunity to remind students that not getting what you want doesn't always mean a situation is unfair (Figure 7–5).

## IMMEDIATE ENVIRONMENTS

Each year I have worked in a classroom, I have taught students with disabilities or who receive services such as speech or occupational therapy. Every day, there are other adults who come in and out of the

FIGURE 7–5 Equal Versus Fair chart

room to either work with students during full-class activities, or who pull students out for individualized supports. Naturally, the comings and goings of certain students and different teachers piques the curiosity of the rest of the class, and there is always a student who asks, "Why do those kids get to go with that teacher?"

This is an opportune moment to revisit the concepts of *equitable* and *equal*, and that there are parts of people's identities that are seen and unseen. As it is not legal or ethical to share students' personal information, I use myself as an example and tell my students that when I was in elementary school, I needed additional help with math. Once a week, I would work with a teacher after school. I explain to my students that not everyone got to work with this teacher, but she helped me because I needed something different in order to be successful in the class. I excelled in other subjects and skills, but I required a particular kind of support in this area. After this conversation, sometimes my students who receive services proudly share that one teacher helps them with handwriting, and another teacher helps them talk about their feelings. While it may seem small, this normalizes talking about disabilities, and how different people need different types of support.

## SCHOOL TRIPS

Even in preschool, young children are constantly bombarded with biased messages that can have lasting consequences if left unchecked. Meanwhile, exposure to ABAR discussions can equip children with language that empowers them to speak up for themselves and others in the face of injustice. First-grade teacher Naomi O'Brien (she/her) referred to a class trip to see a performance of *The Nutcracker* to discuss issues of identity and representation:

> After seeing *The Nutcracker* at a performing arts center, we discussed the importance of representation. We reflected on who was represented during the performance and how that made us feel. We also discussed who was not represented. The students that saw themselves reflected in the dancers felt happy and said it made them see that they could be dancers too. The students that did not see themselves enjoyed the show but said they felt sad to realize that no one looked like them. They didn't think it was fair. This helped the other students who *were* represented realize that even though things were great for them, they needed to consider the feelings and realities of their classmates and keep other perspectives in mind. It helped them start to notice diversity and representation, or a lack thereof, and call attention to it.

It's been a while since most of us were kids but remember that children are extremely capable and curious. ABAR work in the classroom can have a drastic impact on student culture. O'Brien noted both the short- and long-term impact of engaging her students in this work. She observed that her students became more comfortable valuing and accepting diversity and wanted to find ways to fight examples of injustice. "They choose books to intentionally learn about people that are different from them. They are supportive of the different languages, foods, traditions, and customs their friends have. They find different cultures exciting and interesting, not 'weird.'"

## CURRENT EVENTS

In fall 2018, I was teaching third grade in the midst of the #MeToo movement. It didn't seem appropriate to discuss sexual relationships or harassment with eight- and nine-year-olds, but I wanted to teach skills my students would need when they got older in order to avoid creating or finding themselves in situations like the ones circulating on the news. With my students, we talked about safe physical interactions that occur daily in the classroom and outside at recess, and how to communicate your personal boundaries with those around you. We began by defining the word *consent* and broke it down to its simplest form. We talked about what it means to give someone permission to do something. The group landed on the definition "To say yes or no to something, and to be allowed to do something." As a class, we co-created the anchor chart in Figure 7–6 and discussed situations when you need to give or ask for consent and how you can express discomfort. I also wanted my third graders to explore the

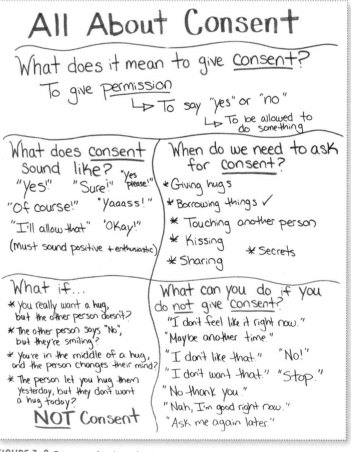

FIGURE 7–6 Consent Anchor chart

gray areas, like if someone allows a physical interaction one day but doesn't want it the next, or if someone says no but they look like they're joking. The conversations were age appropriate, and we were able to tackle this grown-up, real-world issue from a proactive stance.

When it came to teaching my students about Black Lives Matter, it was challenging to figure out how, in an elementary school class, to summarize centuries of historical oppression, racist laws and ideologies, and unbalanced systems of power. Rather than assigning my students pages of reading, we began by analyzing images and pairing them with thinking routines such as "See, Think, Wonder." In this example in

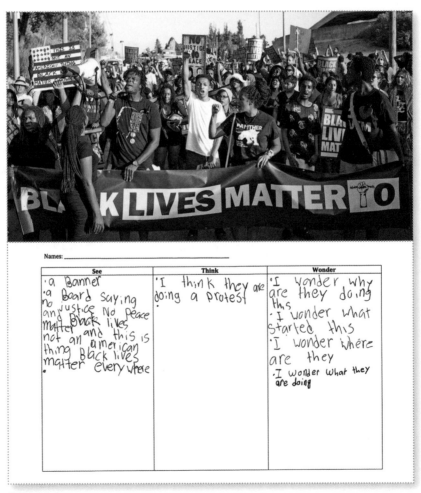

FIGURE 7-7 See, Think, Wonder chart on Black Lives Matter

Figure 7–7, pairs of students were asked to write about what they objectively saw in the photo, what they thought was happening, and what the photo made them wonder. They shared their thinking with their partners before writing anything down.

## } KEEP IN MIND {

"If we are not having these conversations, we are not honoring who children are as learners. We are not honoring where they are developmentally. Because of the way children construct knowledge, they're looking to make connections, and how they're trying to understand their world. If children aren't having conversations that are thoughtful with adults who are helping them understand what is racist, what is inequitable, and systemic issues of oppression that we live in, then they're going to fill in the blanks themselves, and they're not going to necessarily make correct connections. They're going to be taking what they see at the surface level within our society and culture, and draw conclusions for themselves."

—ANNA HINDLEY (SHE/HER)

# Creating a Sustainable Practice: The Gradual Release of Responsibility

When I was in school for my teaching credentials and master's degree, we studied the psychologist Lev Vygotsky and his work on sociocultural theory. Vygotsky described a *Zone of Proximal Development* (graphic in Figure 7–8), or "the distance between the actual developmental level as determined by independent problem-solving and the level of potential development as determined through problem-solving under adult guidance, or in collaboration with more capable peers" (Vygotsky 1978, 86). While this concept is commonly applied to supporting students in academic subjects and skills, I was curious to see what my young students were capable of comprehending when exploring and discussing ABAR

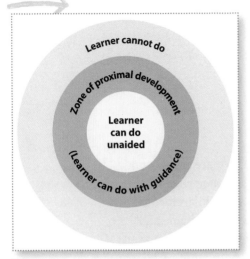

Learner cannot do

Zone of proximal development

Learner
can do
unaided

(Learner can do with guidance)

FIGURE 7-8 Zone of Proximal Development

topics independently, and what they could do with guidance. I knew that my students could use ABAR vocabulary words such as *privilege* or *equitable* with prompting in class or by referencing the word wall, but what kinds of opportunities was I creating for students to take ownership of their learning and express their ideas in their own words?

## How Do I Know If It's Working?

One of my favorite ways to assess understanding with learners is to have them interact with a new text or media such as a contemporary TV show or film. I ask them to identify ABAR themes and appropriately apply the language we learned in class. In recent years, I have started showing my students the 2016 animated film *Zootopia* (Howard and Moore 2016) and ask them to write a reflective essay about examples of prejudice, bias, and power they observed in the film. As an extension of the lesson, students identify media that push back against stereotypes and portray characters from a multidimensional perspective. With younger students, it's just as easy to watch small clips from the film and ask them to say aloud or write one word about what they notice.

Balance studying injustice by also holding space to discuss what justice and liberation could look like. In class, we look at examples of what countries have done to right their wrongs, such as South Africa creating the Truth and Reconciliation Commission, and the Allied forces holding the Nuremberg Trials (as part of our fourth-grade Holocaust study). We discuss solutions that will help our own communities heal. In Figure 7–9, students are asked to reflect on the ABAR topics we've learned about, and how they imagine justice for people who have been marginalized and oppressed. While there is no ideal example of how communities have sought to repair harm they have caused, we have to remind our young learners that we must always have hope, and believe in people's ability to learn, grow, and change.

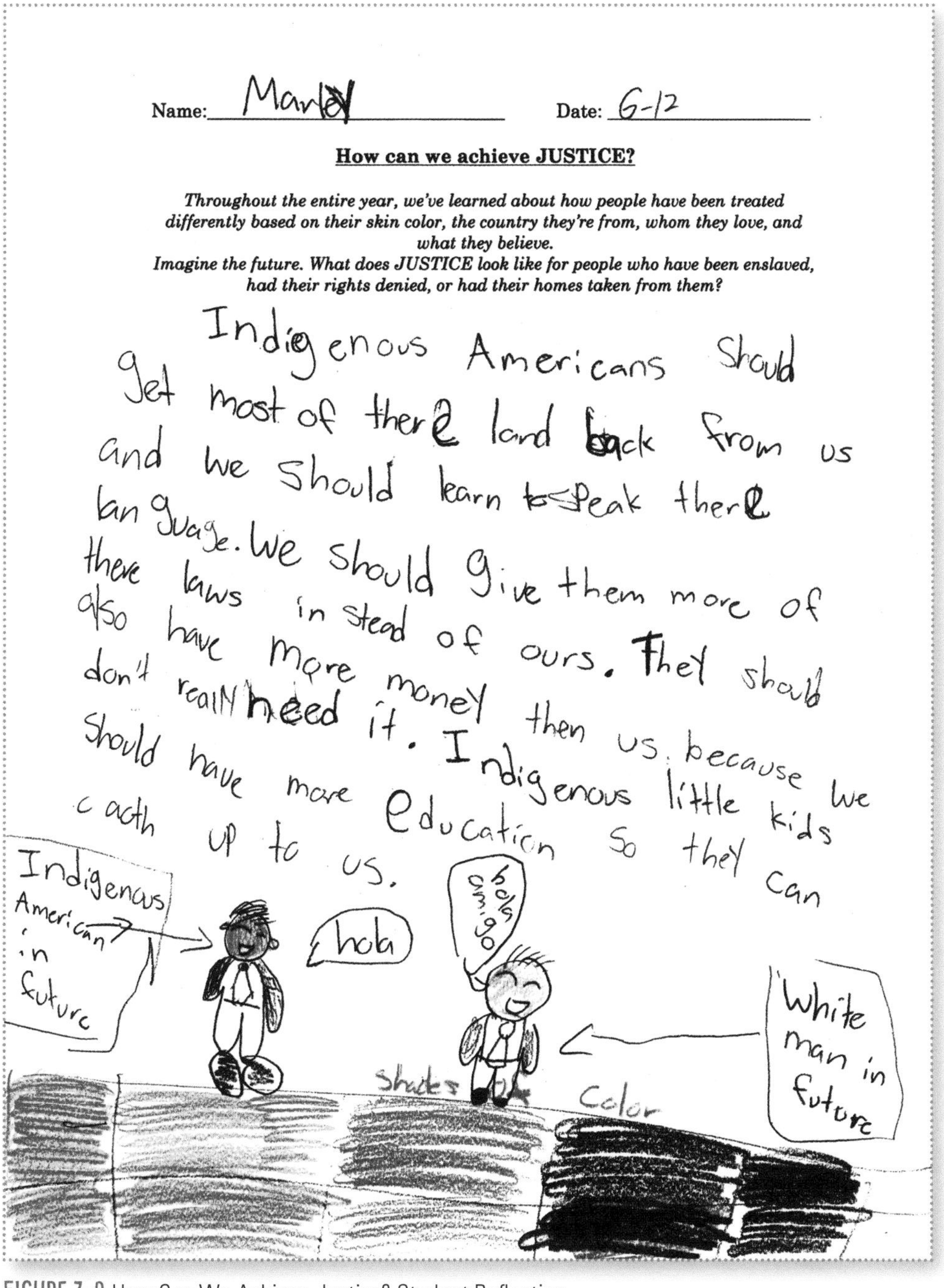

Name: Marley     Date: 6-12

## How can we achieve JUSTICE?

*Throughout the entire year, we've learned about how people have been treated differently based on their skin color, the country they're from, whom they love, and what they believe.*
*Imagine the future. What does JUSTICE look like for people who have been enslaved, had their rights denied, or had their homes taken from them?*

Indigenous Americans should get most of there land back from us and we should learn to speak there language. We should give them more of there laws instead of ours. They should also have more money then us. because we don't really need it. Indigenous little kids should have more education so they can cacth up to us.

Indigenous American in future →

hola

hola amigo

shades   color   White man in future

FIGURE 7–9 How Can We Achieve Justice? Student Reflection

## Don't Reinvent the Wheel

While you might find more ABAR resources geared toward middle and upper grades, we've seen an expanded number of books and organizations dedicated to supporting early childhood and elementary-aged learners. For years, my go-to texts were *Teaching/Learning Anti-Racism: A Developmental Approach*, by Carol Brunson Phillips and Louise Derman-Sparks, and *Anti-Bias Education for Young Children and Ourselves*, by Louise Derman-Sparks and Julie Olsen Edwards. My collection of resources now also includes the following:

» *Rethinking Elementary Education*, edited by Linda Christensen, Mark Hansen, Bob Peterson, Elizabeth Schlessman, and Dyan Watson

» the conscious kid (organization and social media platform)

» EmbraceRace (organization)

» Dismantling Racism (organization)

» Learning for Justice's Social Justice Standards (curriculum)

» Teaching for Change (organization)

# { 8 }

# What Does ABAR Look Like If I Teach STEM Subjects?

**START HERE**

## "I'M JUST NOT A MATH PERSON."

This was my motto from around fourth grade to the beginning of my teaching career. I can pinpoint the moment when my class started to learn long division, and none of the steps made sense. Quickly I learned to memorize certain steps and mimic what my classmates were doing, but I couldn't explain what I was doing or why I was doing it. Then came sixth grade when looking at numbers felt like reading foreign language. My math teacher scolded me in the middle of class and accused me of not paying attention because I consistently made mistakes. My feelings toward math quickly became a gatekeeper, meaning something that prevented me from accessing opportunities or experiences (I openly admit that the graduate school I attended was even more appealing when I learned it did not require GRE test scores to apply). In my years as a teacher, I've lost count of the number of students and adults who I have heard utter these same words. We often let the "I'm not a math or science person" admission slide in ways that we would never accept if a student proclaimed, "I'm just not a reading or writing person," and the messages that grade schools and colleges send echo this sentiment. Some states require fewer math classes than ELA classes to graduate high school, and many colleges and universities do not have a STEM requirement (or have broad subject area requirements such as logic or humanities-based social sciences that allow students to avoid taking STEM classes). What messages are we sending to our students about the importance of STEM in our everyday lives?

Dr. Angela Chan Turrou (she/her) of UCLA's Teacher Education Program conducts research and instructs educators in developing their mathematics methods practice. She reminds teachers to reject the idea that STEM subjects are inherently neutral. "It's true that two plus two will always equal four," she said, "but we have to think about how math in particular is played out for certain folks, how it has served as a gatekeeper, how it has served as a way of limiting particular opportunities to certain kinds of academic and economic endeavors. I think about the ways that education has played out for certain groups of students and how it serves to marginalize and oppress particular demographics in historical, social, economic, and political ways. ABAR in mathematics is important because it means recognizing that there's an inequitable system currently in existence and we need to strive to be educators who are seeking to transform or disrupt that system."

Chris Widmaier (he/him), who taught science in Rochester City School District and currently teaches at Rochester Institute of Technology, describes teaching science as a way for students to practice being decision-makers and looking at how their actions can influence decisions. "It's not just about facts that you need to learn. That mentality is very much like the industrial model of education with a teacher talking while standing in front of the classroom, and it's disempowering for students. ABAR science instruction starts with creating classrooms that are organized for students to have social empowerment, and opportunities to work, learn, communicate, and collaborate together." Widmaier echoed Dr. Turrou's sentiments about the lack of neutrality in teaching science:

> The bias is everywhere. But that's one of the hardest things for science and math teachers. They have this false belief that somehow there's some neutrality in what they do. And nothing is neutral. Bias comes in. It's a false statement to say, "I can't teach about social justice, because the science

curriculum dictates that I only teach these topics and standards." That's just not true. For example, if you're going to teach about vaccines, you can talk about experiments that have been done on people to test vaccines without their knowledge, but you still teach about what a vaccine is, and why they're important. Equity practices in science give better access and introduce diverse ways of engaging with science content, science methods, and making things inquiry based and student centered.

Bob Moses, civil rights activist and author of *Radical Equations* (2001), describes mathematics as a tool of liberation. As a math teacher in New York in the 1980s, Moses noticed that students of color from under-resourced backgrounds were not expected to perform well in math. When he became a MacArthur Fellow, he created the Algebra Project, which strives to create systemic changes in mathematics instruction. "In today's world, economic access and full citizenship depend crucially on math and science literacy," Moses states (Wilgoren 2001, 4). Mathematics is present throughout our entire lives, and access and understanding can transform lives. When we consider what constitutes a social justice curriculum, students must look at the implications of socioeconomic and political policies, and analyze data and use it to support their hypotheses of ongoing issues in our world. How can one truly understand how systemic racism operates without an understanding of numbers? Financial literacy is also a key component in a social justice math curriculum. We are impacted by our accessibility or inaccessibility to money every day of our lives. How can students from low-income communities hope to gain financial independence and stability without an understanding of how money works?

Similarly, it is just as necessary to present the sciences from diverse perspectives (the only notable nonwhite person in STEM I remember learning about as a child was George Washington Carver and his work with peanuts). Middle school science teacher Ace Schwarz (they/them) shared that every year, their students study overlooked scientists in our history. To begin, they ask their students to name three scientists. Schwarz noticed that students rarely name off the top of their heads individuals who aren't white men. They've seen students share more diverse scientists recently, but Schwarz believes many of the gaps in diversity stem from the centralization of white male contributions in science curricula. Director Theodore Melfi's 2016 film *Hidden Figures* reminded the public of overlooked and marginalized individuals such as Katherine Johnson, whose brilliance contributed to scientific gains in our world. It's important for science educators to teach beyond Western classics and consider the discoveries and contributions of Black, Indigenous, Latinx, and Asian cultures and individuals. Environmental science also requires inclusion, as Black and Brown communities of the global south are impacted by climate change at rates far higher than white and Western cities and countries. Inequity in the field of science has led to the displacement of Western Asian refugees and Indigenous peoples of the Americas, illnesses of Black Americans due to pollution and toxic dumping, and the lack of access to healthcare for LGBTQ+ individuals and those who reside in under-resourced neighborhoods.

I've often wondered why mathematics appears to be a more challenging and less approachable subject than English or history. STEM concepts occur everywhere in our world—from the symmetry of snowflakes to architecture, city planning, the technology that powers our phones and computers, and the medicine that keeps us alive. Educators often confine ABAR teaching to reading, writing, and history; yet incorporating social justice into STEM subjects matters not only to equity in general but also plays a crucial role in paying the education debt (Ladson-Billings 2006) owed to students from under-resourced backgrounds. A major aspect of cultivating culturally responsive classroom communities is to create opportunities for our students to see themselves within the content they study. Often this looks like building a diverse classroom library and inviting students to write about their experiences and interests, but it is just as important for students to see how they can take on the roles of mathematicians, scientists, engineers, and innovators in their everyday lives.

# Setting Yourself Up for Success: Examine and Redefine STEM Success

When teachers approach content from an ABAR lens, we have to break down the content itself, as well as our teaching strategies. If you're a

STEM educator whose classroom has operated along traditional structures and instruction, teaching from an equitable and inclusive perspective can feel like an enormous change, but there are small steps to take in order to shift your classroom culture. Dr. Turrou encourages teachers to start examining and redefining what success looks like in a STEM classroom.

> A really simple kind of illustration is to start by thinking about more traditional ways of teaching math, and what we want to change. There's immense power in telling students that you're curious about the way they think. Traditionally how you were successful in math was you memorized formulas, you spout it off, and memorize facts at a high speed. If you were not someone who participated like that, then automatically you were kind of positioned as you are not a math person, and you never will be one, which you then internalize. We have to reflect upon the ways in which teachers have built classroom environments that create a very narrow way of being successful, that's reflective of that kind of broader discourse of what counted as math. There's a lot of current changes with things like understanding that 21st century skills are not just about memorizing numbers or facts. It's about really understanding numerical relationships, being part of a discourse community where you're explaining your thinking, and you're responding and critiquing someone else's thinking, and you're engaging in mathematical argumentation.

Our classroom culture and environment set the tone for whether our students will feel comfortable participating and engaging in the STEM fields. If mistakes are really necessary to push forward in scientific discoveries, how are teachers communicating and modeling how mistakes are expected, inspected, and respected? Are students treated like empty vessels to be filled with division algorithms and the elements of the periodic table, or are students experimenting, working collaboratively, and forming their own knowledge? Do we value and praise diversity of thought, or just the first student who arrives at the correct answer?

**} KEEP IN MIND {**

"For too many students of color, white teachers can be just
another point of 'white authority' in their lives, especially if
their experiences, voices, and perspectives aren't valued."
—MOLLY TANSEY AND MELISSA KATZ (2015, 4)

## Consider How You Teach Content-Specific Language

Language shapes the way we think, and humans struggle to understand concepts that we do not have the words to describe. New York–
based teacher and activist José Vilson (he/him) noticed that some of
his Latinx students were struggling with the concept of place value.
He drew on his students' native languages and carried it into his math
instruction. "In the interest of financial literacy, I do like to use money,
because there's this really neat word in Spanish called *centavo*. I'll say,
well, what's a *centavo*? It's a penny, right? And then what is it that that
will do? Well, if I gather one hundred centavos, I get a dollar. Oh, but
there's a word within centavo that I kind of recognize. And that's that
prefix, *cent*, that root word. And once I start plugging into that conversation, it becomes, 'Wait, I've seen that word before,' and I can pull it
into percentages. Then we start building the term *percent* based on
what they already know, in the context and the languages that they
already have."

As STEM educators, we must consider our approaches to
teaching content-specific language and vocabulary. Are we teaching
the language of math with the same precision that we use in teaching reading and writing? Particularly with students who are emerging
bilinguals, we cannot take the definitions of STEM-specific terms for
granted. Every year, my class has a discussion about how the word
*equal* means *the same as*, and we list synonyms such as *plus* and *add*.
Consider making developmentally appropriate and grade-specific anchor charts—of synonyms, antonyms, prefixes and suffixes—in math
and science.

## Use Your Curriculum or Standards to Your Advantage

The organization Radical Math (www.radicalmath.org) reminds teachers, "Find an issue that fits the math, not the other way around. When you try to make the math fit an issue you want to cover, most likely, you will end up sacrificing some of the mathematical content" (2007). One of the barriers I perceived when I first ventured into ABAR in STEM was how inaccessible real-world numbers felt. It was easy to find a differentiated text on a particular subject, or create a writing prompt that all students could connect with, but if I was using math and science to teach about current events and social issues, it didn't feel right to make up figures for the sake of the lesson. As much as I might want to dig into government budgets or teach about how credit card interest rates work, certain topics didn't quite fit the concepts my students needed to understand. Try to look at the main concepts and standards covered in your scope and sequence for the year and plug in topics that fit into what students will need to understand. Figure 8–1 shows a possible list of STEM topics with corresponding ABAR topics.

FIGURE 8–1 STEM and Corresponding ABAR Topics

| STEM Topic | ABAR Corresponding Topic |
|---|---|
| Measurement and conversion | Students study transportation routes and calculate the time and distance between different locations in their community, and make recommendations on how to increase efficiency. |
| Representation of data through graphs | Students create surveys around different social issues, poll their classmates, and represent their findings. |
| Geometry | Students study geometric artwork and designs of different cultures, such as origami and mandalas. |
| Engineering and design | Students study the geography of their community and identify the location of resources. Students then study city planning to redesign their community in a way that creates more access to resources for all residents. |

## Make a Plan to Connect STEM to Students' Lives

When it comes to the content itself, devote time to auditing your curriculum for diverse perspectives as well as real-world applications. Can all of your students see themselves reflected in STEM subjects across their social identities, and can you create opportunities for students to learn about inventors and creators of identities different from their own? Some of my favorite lessons to teach feature individuals such as Sophie Germain, Alan Turing, and Mae Jemison, as well as the discoveries made by Indigenous and Western Asian civilizations. However, reflecting on my own identity as a student in math and science, I cannot recall learning about a single famous individual who looked like me.

Many STEM classes are guided by textbooks that are adopted by schools or entire districts, and classes often require teachers to put in additional time for extensive preparation and collecting materials. (I have personally spent hours reading over science lessons from my school's curriculum, making runs to Home Depot to make sure each student had access to enough materials, and poking my head into my colleagues' classrooms to borrow a few extra rulers or thermometers.) Prescribed curricula and textbooks are teaching tools and can offer students and teachers access to background information, as well as a scope and sequence and pacing guide for teaching certain topics. Becoming an ABAR-focused STEM teacher does not mean we abandon teaching concepts like subtraction and the water cycle. It simply means that we shift the lens through which we teach our content.

When you plan ahead for your STEM units, I find it helpful to consider each topic through the perspectives of diversity, equity, and inclusion. Am I representing diverse perspectives and contributions in this field? Are my students learning about how this topic can be used to create an equitable society, or how it has been misused as a way to promote oppression? Are my teaching strategies inclusive for all learners? Figure 8–2 is a STEM planner I use. Notice how I start with the standards and think my way across diversity, equity, and inclusion. You'll find a blank template for this form in the online resources.

STEM Planner

OR 8–1

| | Diversity (Who is being represented? How can I elevate the contributions of diverse individuals and groups?) | Equity (What are and have been the practical and equitable/ inequitable applications?) | Inclusion (What strategies am I using to meet the needs of my learners?) |
|---|---|---|---|
| **Science (NGSS)** **3-LS3-2 Heredity: Inheritance and Variation of Traits** Use evidence to support the explanation that traits can be influenced by the environment. (Grades 3–5) | ■ Harriet Creighton was a botanist and geneticist. She discovered "jumping genes" and was the first female solo scientist to be awarded the Nobel Prize in physiology. ■ Dr. James E. Bowman was the first Black professor in the University of Chicago's Biological Sciences Division. He studied inherited diseases. He spoke out against mandatory sickle cell screenings and believed they could be used to reinforce racist ideas. | ■ Skin color is determined by melanin, living in proximity to the equator, and inheritance from our ancestors, but this trait has been used as a reason to discriminate against people with dark skin. ■ The peppered moth physically evolved during the industrial revolution due to human-created environmental changes such as pollution. | ■ Sorting and matching traits with pictures of different environments to support hands-on learning. ■ Clearly defining vocabulary words for all students, but especially emerging bilingual students. |
| **Technology (ISTE)** *Knowledge Constructor (3b)* Students critically curate a variety of resources using digital tools to construct knowledge, produce creative artifacts, and make meaningful learning experiences for themselves and others. Students evaluate the accuracy, perspective, credibility and relevance of information, media, data or other resources. (K–12) | ■ Tarana Burke created the MeToo campaign as a way to connect with other survivors of sexual assault. The movement was publicized on social media under the hashtag #MeToo. ■ Alicia Garza, Patrisse Cullors, and Opal Tometi created the Black Lives Matter movement in response to the shooting of Trayvon Martin in 2013, and the persistence of police violence against Black people. Black Lives Matter is now a global network with over forty chapters worldwide. | ■ Analysis of "fake news" and media bias. There have been a number of stories in the media about their impact on our political elections, as well as divisions in our society. Can students discern factual news from fake news? ■ What is the outcome of governments that restrict the use of media and are able to control what information is available to citizens? | ■ Offer opportunities to practice practical tech skills like typing (how to capitalize, indent, etc.). Just because students play games on computers doesn't mean they know how to type or identify reliable online sources. ■ Survey students to learn about what kinds of tech they have access to at home, and how these are used. |
| **Engineering (NGSS)** *K-2-ETS1-1* Ask questions, make observations, and gather information about a situation people want to change to define a simple problem that can be solved through the development of a new or improved object or tool. (Grade 2) | ■ At eight years old, Mexican child activist and scientist Xóchitl Guadalupe Cruz built a solar-powered water heater from recyclable materials in order to create better access to hot water for people who live in rural areas. ■ Hans Jørgen Wiberg, a visually impaired Danish furniture craftsman, created an app to help other visually impaired people around the world. The Be My Eyes app connects blind and low-vision people with sighted volunteers or company representatives for visual assistance through a live video. | ■ More than twenty countries in Africa have committed to building a Great Green Wall of trees and vegetation across the continent in order to combat the spread of the Sahara Desert, climate change, drought, and food scarcity. | ■ Consider the socioeconomic backgrounds of your students when assigning projects. If students are given homework assignments or asked to participate in science fairs, are they expected to purchase materials themselves or are these provided? ■ Grade projects and assignments with rubrics to encourage open-ended questions and creative strategies. |
| **Mathematics (CCSS)** CCSS.MATH.CONTENT.4.OA.A.3 Solve multistep word problems posed with whole numbers and having whole-number answers using the four operations, including problems in which remainders must be interpreted. Represent these problems using equations with a letter standing for the unknown quantity. Assess the reasonableness of answers using mental computation and estimation strategies including rounding. (Grade 4) | ■ Sophie Germain was a French mathematician born in 1776 who made important contributions to number theory. Due to discrimination against women in math, she used the pseudonym "Leblanc" in order to share her work. ■ Shiing-Shen Chern, a Chinese American mathematician and poet, was one of the most famous leaders in geometry. | ■ Observe the timetables of local public transportation methods and determine how the schedules may impact people without access to a personal vehicle. ■ Discuss applications of financial literacy such as shopping budgets, monthly cost of living expenses, etc. | ■ Encourage diversity of thought by asking students, "Did anyone solve this problem a different way?" ■ Offer options for how students can share their answers beyond calling on individual students to speak out, such as partner sharing, writing, or drawing their work. |

FIGURE 8–2 Sample STEM Planner

# Taking Action in the Classroom: Culturally Responsive Practices in STEM

I was always the student in math class who would ask the teacher, "Why are we learning how to find the area of a triangle? When are we going to use this in real life?" There are so many powerful connections between math concepts taught in class and application in the real world, and it's important that our students understand their relevance. If students are learning to add and subtract, why not have them create a grocery budget using coupons and mailers? If we're teaching geometry, why not have them study how buildings are designed and constructed? When we apply mathematical concepts, we have the opportunity to analyze toxic waste sites (as some students did in Figure 8–3), climate change, the ratio of incarcerated people of color to the general population, or simply to understand the nutritional panel on a container of food. With any subject we teach, connections to our students' everyday lives make learning all the more meaningful.

FIGURE 8-3 Students Examine a Map of the Proximity of Toxic Waste Sites to Black Communities in the United States

## Draw a Picture

At the very beginning of the year I give my students a simple task: draw a picture of a mathematician or a scientist. Most students draw a variety of men who resemble Albert Einstein, usually wearing glasses and white coats, and sporting beards. We take notice of the trends we see in our illustrations. As a follow-up activity, I display a number of portraits of people from different eras and backgrounds and ask my students what all of these people have in common (spoiler alert: they're all accomplished in STEM fields!). When I repeat the Draw a Picture activity later on, the follow-up activity completely alters the outcome. My students drew a diverse array of people, and one student even asked, "Can I just draw myself?" See Figure 8–4 for examples of some of their drawings.

## Numbers in Our Daily Lives

Start by brainstorming about everything kids know about math and where numbers occur in their daily lives. You might hear things like, "How far you drive to school," and "The temperature outside," or "Days until my birthday." It excites them to share all of the ways that numbers are visible and the ways they naturally use math, and our list grows.

FIGURE 8–4 Student Drawings of Mathematicians

After you brainstorm, think about how you can connect your curriculum to what students already know about numbers in their lives. Go back to the STEM planner in Figure 8–2 if you need additional support.

When I taught fourth grade, our multiplication unit took on a new form as we studied the cost of living in Los Angeles by comparing the minimum wage to the average rent in different neighborhoods. We researched real job postings, and my students were appalled to learn that working full-time, entry-level jobs would not bring in enough income to pay rent, utilities, and food. We added on hourly raises of less than one dollar and graphed how our income would grow over time. Figure 8–5 introduces and summarizes the unit, while also stating the CCSS covered and assessed, while Figures 8–6 and 8–7 show how students calculated their income based on an hourly wage, and cost of living.

Toward the end of the year we focused on financial literacy and invited community members to visit our class and talk about how bank accounts and credit cards work, what it's like to own a business, and how to calculate expenses, revenue, and profit. I noticed that my students were not only engaged but invested in these lessons. When they discussed the problems, they would often use first-person language, which reflected how they saw themselves in the problem-solving process.

Name: _Pav)_

### Social Justice Math: Living in Los Angeles

Los Angeles is an amazing place to live, but it is also one of the most expensive cities in the United States. For this project, we will consider the cost of living in Los Angeles based on average rent, transportation, utilities, and more, and study the minimum wage in order to learn what it takes to live in this city.

#### 4th Grade Common Core Math Standards Covered:

CCSS.MATH.CONTENT.4.OA.A.1

Interpret a multiplication equation as a comparison, e.g., interpret 35 = 5 × 7 as a statement that 35 is 5 times as many as 7 and 7 times as many as 5. Represent verbal statements of multiplicative comparisons as multiplication equations.

CCSS.MATH.CONTENT.4.OA.A.2

Multiply or divide to solve word problems involving multiplicative comparison, e.g., by using drawings and equations with a symbol for the unknown number to represent the problem, distinguishing multiplicative comparison from additive comparison.1

CCSS.MATH.CONTENT.4.OA.A.3

Solve multistep word problems posed with whole numbers and having whole-number answers using the four operations, including problems in which remainders must be interpreted. Represent these problems using equations with a letter standing for the unknown quantity. Assess the reasonableness of answers using mental computation and estimation strategies including rounding.

CCSS.MATH.CONTENT.4.NBT.B.5

Multiply a whole number of up to four digits by a one-digit whole number, and multiply two two-digit numbers, using strategies based on place value and the properties of operations. Illustrate and explain the calculation by using equations, rectangular arrays, and/or area models.

FIGURE 8–5 Financial Literacy Project

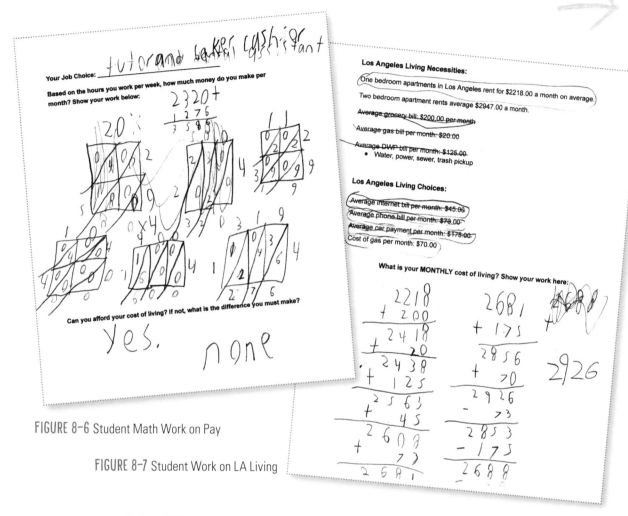

FIGURE 8-6 Student Math Work on Pay

FIGURE 8-7 Student Work on LA Living

Other STEM educators have found success by tying in current events and personal experiences to their curriculum. Ace Schwarz created a unit on the events of Arab Spring in the early 2010s in order to take a different perspective on teaching climate change. They also expanded their human biology lessons to be inclusive of LGBTQ+ students and narratives by teaching about the difference between sex, gender, and gender expression.

José Vilson recounted his favorite equity-focused math unit on Dr. Martin Luther King Jr. and the March on Washington, where he took a unit on data and linear relationships and had his middle school students study job percentages and economic disparities as evidence for why people were marching in the streets of the capital.

Chris Widmaier also described how he considered the importance of helping students to understand the ways that science has been misused to reinforce systems of racism and bias.

> *The biggest example is that the whole idea of race was constructed by the scientists back in the 1700s and 1800s to justify slavery. They needed a way to fix that cognitive dissonance they had about the fact that despite being Christians, they were treating people terribly. As a solution, they had to come up with scientific reasons that proved white people were superior to everybody else. Once we started talking about these things in class, we could also discuss the history of how we got to where we are with racism, and the role that science has played. It's a really important, overlooked idea, but we have to examine things like the Tuskegee experiments, how that was another example of an injustice that has been perpetuated against Black people with the support of the scientific community. While those are some examples of things that I try to teach, the other part is to empower students and communities with scientific knowledge and then to be able to recognize what's going on in the world around them. I want them to be able to use the scientific method to collect evidence and provide evidence-based claims for what's happening around them. Students need to be able to look at issues that might be using science to fuel discrimination in order to recognize and combat them and use science as a tool of empowerment to make the world better.*

# Creating a Sustainable Practice: Make Sure Students Connect STEM to Their Lives and Community

Looking back at my experience as a math student, I recognize that one reason I had difficulty engaging with the subject matter is because the *why* was often missing. I remember wondering why we had to learn the quadratic formula, and when I would ever need to calculate the area of an isosceles triangle. When I asked one of my math teachers when in life I would need to graph linear equations, the question was brushed off. I wasn't trying to have an attitude, I was genuinely curious about when I would need algebra in my life outside of school.

## How Do I Know If It's Working?

To ensure that students understand the connection between classroom learning and learning outside of school, we can continue to circle back to the idea that STEM subjects help us find solutions to problems in our communities. One way we can identify whether students are making the connection is to ask them how STEM could be used to better understand and solve problems in our communities. Brainstorm about community issues and concerns and ask STEM-oriented questions like:

>> What numbers do we see as we learn about this issue?

>> How can numbers help us understand more?

>> What questions can we ask that involve numbers?

>> How can we use numbers to help us find a solution?

>> How can we use numbers to teach other people about this issue?

Another way to know whether your approach to STEM is working is to ask students for feedback in a quarterly survey. Ask simple questions like "Is STEM important in your life? Why? What have you learned?" Compare answers over time to see if student responses change or stay the same. Here are some third-grade student responses:

>> "I see that more Black people are put in jail more than other groups. This makes me wonder why."

>> "I see that the number of homeless people in LA got a lot bigger than last year and the year before that. I didn't know how big."

>> "I learned that living in LA is really expensive and people have to work lots of hours to live here and have things they need."

START HERE, START NOW

>> "We can use numbers to count how many people have stuff or don't have stuff and when we see more even numbers we can learn that things are maybe better?"

>> "We can use numbers to teach lots of things because the whole world has numbers."

## Don't Reinvent the Wheel

While ABAR resources for humanities may be more visible to educators, there are a number of publications and organizations dedicated to supporting this lens in STEM fields. Additionally, don't discount general STEM resources that can be used as inspiration and guidance in developing your own projects and units of study.

>> *Rethinking Mathematics*, edited by Eric Gutstein and Bob Peterson

>> *Radical Equations*, by Robert P. Moses and Charles E. Cobb Jr.

>> *Mathematical Mindsets,* by Jo Boaler

>> "Indigenous Knowledge and Science Revisited," by Glen S. Aikenhead and Masakata Ogawa

>> *Children's Mathematics*, by Thomas Carpenter et al.

>> *Choral Counting & Counting Collections: Transforming the PreK–5 Math Classroom*, by Megan L. Franke, Elham Kazemi, and Angela Chan Turrou

>> *Young Children's Mathematics: Cognitively Guided Instruction in Early Childhood Education*, by Thomas Carpenter et al.

>> Black Girls Code, www.blackgirlscode.com

>> UCLA Mathematics Project, https://centerx.gseis.ucla.edu/math-project

>> Radical Math, www.radicalmath.org/main.php?id=Social JusticeMath

>> National Council of Teachers of Mathematics, www.nctm.org/

>> *Focusing Science and Engineering Learning on Justice-Centered Phenomena Across PK–12*, by Deb Morrison, Philip Bell, and Abby Rhinehart

# WORKS CITED

Abdin-Adnani, Razan. 2018. "Planting the Seeds for a New World: Cultivating an Anti-Bias, Anti-Racist Home." *AMI/USA Journal* (Spring). https://amiusa.org/planting-the-seeds-for-a-new-world-cultivating-an-anti-bias-anti-racist-home.

Ada, Alma Flor. 1997. *The Lizard and the Sun*. New York: Dragonfly Books.

Adichie, Chimamanda Ngozi. "The Danger of a Single Story." Filmed October 2009. TED video, 18:33. www.ted.com/talks/chimamanda_ngozi_adichie_the_danger_of_a_single_story/transcript?language=en.

Aikenhead, Glen S., and Masakata Ogawa. 2007. "Indigenous Knowledge and Science Revisited." *Cultural Studies of Science Education* 2: 539–620.

Amatea, Ellen S. 2013. *Building Culturally Responsive Family–School Relationships*. 2nd ed. Boston: Pearson.

Arab American National Museum. https://arabamericanmuseum.org.

Black Girls Code. www.blackgirlscode.com.

Boaler, Jo. 2016. *Mathematical Mindsets: Unleashing Students' Potential Through Creative Math, Inspiring Messages and Innovative Teaching*. San Francisco: Jossey-Bass.

Bronson, Po, and Ashley Merryman. 2009. *NurtureShock: New Thinking About Children*. New York: Twelve.

Brown, Brené. 2020. *The Gifts of Imperfection*. New York: Random House.

Carpenter, Thomas P., Elizabeth Fennema, Megan Loef Franke, Linda Levi, and Susan B. Empson. 2014. *Children's Mathematics: Cognitively Guided Instruction*. 2nd ed. Portsmouth, NH: Heinemann.

Carpenter, Thomas P., Megan Loef Franke, Nicholas C. Johnson, Angela C. Turrou, and Anita A. Wager. 2016. *Young Children's Mathematics: Cognitively Guided Instruction in Early Childhood Education*. Portsmouth, NH: Heinemann.

Castree, Noel, Rob Kitchin, and Alisdair Rogers. 2013. *Oxford Dictionary of Human Geography*. Oxford, UK: Oxford University Press. https://www.oxfordreference.com/view/10.1093/acref/9780199599868.001.0001/acref-9780199599868-e-975.

Christensen, Linda, Mark Hansen, Bob Peterson, Elizabeth Schlessman, and Dyan Watson, eds. 2012. *Rethinking Elementary Education*. Milwaukee, WI: Rethinking Schools.

Climo, Shirley. 1993. *The Korean Cinderella*. Illustrated by Ruth Heller. New York: HarperCollins.

*Code Switch* (podcast). www.npr.org/sections/codeswitch.

Common Core State Standards Initiative (CCSSI). 2021. *Common Core State Standards*. Washington, DC: National Governors Association (NGA) and Council of Chief State School Officers (CCSSO). http://www.corestandards.org/.

the conscious kid. www.theconsciouskid.org.

Constantino, Steven M. 2021. *Engage Every Family: Five Simple Principles*. 2nd ed. Thousand Oaks, CA: Corwin.

Crenshaw, Kimberlé. 1989. "Demarginalizing the Intersection of Race and Sex: A Black Feminist Critique of Antidiscrimination Doctrine, Feminist Theory and Antiracist Politics." *The University of Chicago Legal Forum* 1989 (1): Article 8. http://chicagounbound.uchicago.edu/uclf/vol1989/iss1/8.

Cummings, Pat. 2002. *Ananse and the Lizard*. New York: Henry Holt and Company.

Derman-Sparks, Louise, and Julie Olsen Edwards. 2020. *Anti-Bias Education for Young Children and Ourselves*. Rev. ed. Washington, DC: National Association for the Education of Young Children.

*Disability After Dark* (podcast). www.andrewgurza.com/podcast.

Dismantling Racism. www.dismantlingracism.org.

Dunbar-Ortiz, Roxanne. 2014. *An Indigenous Peoples' History of the United States*. Boston: Beacon Press.

EmbraceRace. www.embracerace.org.

ESPN. *The Body Issue*. www.espn.com/espn/feature/story/_/id/27400369/the-body-issue.

Evans, Katherine, and Dorothy Vaandering. 2016. *The Little Book of Restorative Justice in Education: Fostering Responsibility, Healing, and Hope in Schools*. New York: Good Books.

Facing History and Ourselves. www.facinghistory.org.

Fariña, Carmen, and Laura Kotch. 2014. *A School Leader's Guide to Excellence.* Updated ed. Portsmouth, NH: Heinemann.

First Nations Education Steering Committee. 2019. *BC First Nations Land, Title, and Governance Teacher Resource Guide—Elementary, Secondary.* West Vancouver, BC: First Nations Education Steering Committee. http://www.fnesc.ca/governance-2.

Forrester, Kate. 2016. *Celtic Tales.* San Francisco: Chronicle Books.

Franke, Megan L, Elham Kazemi, and Angela Chan Turrou. 2018. *Choral Counting & Counting Collections: Transforming the PreK–5 Math Classroom.* Portland, ME: Stenhouse.

Freire, Paulo. (1970) 2018. *Pedagogy of the Oppressed.* 4th ed. New York: Bloomsbury Academic.

*Gender Galaxy.* www.actioncanadashr.org/sites/default/files/2019-03 /Action_Canada_for_Sexual_Health_and_Rights_Beyondthe Basics_Galaxy-web.pdf.

GLSEN Educator Resources. www.glsen.org/resources /educator-resources.

*Good Ancestor Podcast.* http://laylafsaad.com/good-ancestor-podcast.

Gooden, Mark Anthony. 2020. "What an Anti-Racist Principal Must Do." *Education Week Special Report*, October 13. www.edweek.org /leadership/opinion-what-an-anti-racist-principal-must-do/2020/10.

Gorski, Paul. 2019. "Avoiding Racial Equity Detours." *Educational Leadership* 76 (7): 56–61.

Gutstein, Eric, and Bob Peterson, eds. 2013. *Rethinking Mathematics: Teaching Social Justice by the Numbers.* 2nd ed. Milwaukee, WI: Rethinking Schools.

Henderson, Anne T., Karen L. Mapp, Vivian R. Johnson, and Don Davies. 2007. *Beyond the Bake Sale: The Essential Guide to Family–School Partnerships.* New York: The New Press.

Hoffman, Sarah, and Ian Hoffman. 2014. *Jacob's New Dress.* Illustrated by Chris Case. Park Ridge, IL: Albert Whitman and Company.

Howard, Byron, and Rich Moore, dirs. 2016. *Zootopia.* 1 hr. 50 min. Burbank, CA: Walt Disney Studios.

Illuminatives.org (website of Illumi*Native*).

*Intersectionality Matters!* (podcast). https://www.aapf.org /intersectionality-matters.

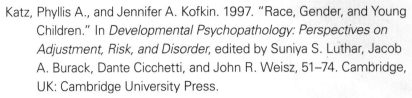

Katz, Phyllis A., and Jennifer A. Kofkin. 1997. "Race, Gender, and Young Children." In *Developmental Psychopathology: Perspectives on Adjustment, Risk, and Disorder*, edited by Suniya S. Luthar, Jacob A. Burack, Dante Cicchetti, and John R. Weisz, 51–74. Cambridge, UK: Cambridge University Press.

Kelly, David J., Paul C. Quinn, Alan M. Slater, Kang Lee, Alan Gibson, Michael Smith, Liezhong Ge, and Olivier Pascalis. 2005. "Three-Months-Olds, but Not Newborns, Prefer Own-Race Faces." *Developmental Science* 8 (6): F31–F36.

Kersey, Sara. 2019. Recorded interview with author, August 21.

Kinzler, Katherine D. 2016. "How Kids Learn Prejudice." *New York Times*, October 23, SR 9. www.nytimes.com/2016/10/23/opinion /sunday/how-kids-learn-prejudice.html.

Kleinrock, Liz. 2019. "How to Teach Kids to Talk About Taboo Topics." Filmed January 2019. TED video, 11:52. www.ted.com/talks/liz _kleinrock_how_to_teach_kids_to_talk_about_taboo_topics ?language=en.

———. 2020. "Anti-Racist Work in Schools: Are You in It for the Long Haul?" June 30, *Learning for Justice*. https://www.learningfor justice.org/magazine/antiracist-work-in-schools-are-you-in-it -for-the-long-haul.

Ladson-Billings, Gloria. 2006. "From the Achievement Gap to the Education Debt: Understanding Achievement in U.S. Schools." *Educational Researcher* 35 (7): 3–12. https://www.jstor.org /stable/3876731.

Learning for Justice. n.d. *Best Practices for Serving LGBTQ Students*. Learning for Justice. www.learningforjustice.org/magazine /publications/best-practices-for-serving-lgbtqstudents?fbclid =IwAR302RzoOqdA7J5a8kJdpHqQDfnLJglVm6UUsJr4Vq M6M2X5enL_HQXY2s0.

———. n.d. *Critical Practices for Anti-bias Education: Family and Community Engagement*. Learning for Justice. www.learningforjustice .org/magazine/publications/critical-practices-for-antibias-education.

———. n.d. *Let's Talk*. Learning for Justice. www.learningforjustice.org /magazine/publications/lets-talk.

———. n.d. *Speak Up at School*. Learning for Justice. www.learningfor justice.org/magazine/publications/speak-up-at-school.

————. n.d. "Social Justice Standards: A Framework for Anti-bias Education." www.learningforjustice.org/frameworks/social-justice-standards.

————. n.d."Teaching Hard History: American Slavery: A Framework for Teaching American Slavery." www.learningforjustice.org/frameworks/teaching-hard-history/american-slavery.

————. n.d. *Teaching Hard History: American Slavery* (podcast and publication). Learning for Justice. www.learningforjustice.org/magazine/publications/teaching-hard-history-american-slavery. www.learningforjustice.org/podcasts/teaching-hard-history.

Lee, Harper. 1960. *To Kill a Mockingbird*. Philadelphia: Lippincott.

Lee and Low Books. www.leeandlow.com.

Lencioni, Patrick. 2002. *The Five Dysfunctions of a Team*. San Francisco: Jossey-Bass.

Lukoff, Kyle. 2009. *When Aidan Became a Brother*. Illustrated by Kaylani Juanita. New York: Lee and Low Books.

Lyon, George Ella. 1999. "Where I'm From." *Where I'm From: Where Poems Come From*. Spring, TX: Absey and Co.

Mapp, Karen L., Ilene Carver, and Jessica Lander. 2017. *Powerful Partnerships: A Teacher's Guide to Engaging Families for Student Success*. New York: Scholastic.

Martin, Rafe. 1992. *The Rough-Face Girl*. Illustrated by David Shannon. New York: G. F. Putnam's Sons.

Melfi, Theodore, dir. 2016. *Hidden Figures*. Los Angeles: 20th Century Fox.

The Mexican Museum. www.mexicanmuseum.org.

Mindell, Arnold. (1995) 2014. *Sitting in the Fire: Large Group Transformation Using Conflict and Diversity*. San Francisco: Deep Democracy Exchange.

Morrison, Deb, Philip Bell, and Abby Rhinehart. 2020. *Focusing Science and Engineering Learning on Justice-Centered Phenomena Across PK–12*. STEM Teaching Tools Practice Brief No. 67. http://stemteachingtools.org/brief/67.

Moses, Robert P., and Charles E. Cobb. 2001. *Radical Equations: Civil Rights from Mississippi to the Algebra Project*. Boston: Beacon Press.

Museum of Tolerance. www.museumoflearningforjustice.com.

National Civil Rights Museum. www.civilrightsmuseum.org.

National Council of Teachers of Mathematics. www.nctm.org.

Next Generation Science Standards (NGSS) Lead States. 2013. *Next Generation Science Standards: For States, By States.* Washington, DC: The National Academies Press. https://www.nextgenscience .org/.

*Nice White Parents* (podcast). www.nytimes.com/2020/07/23/podcasts /nice-white-parents-serial.html.

*Our Words, Our Ways: Teaching First Nations, Métis and Inuit Learners.* 2005. Alberta, Canada: Alberta Education, Aboriginal Services Branch and Teaching Resources Branch. https://education.alberta .ca/media/3615876/our-words-our-ways.pdf.

Parker, Priya. 2018. *The Art of Gathering: How We Meet and Why It Matters.* New York: Riverhead Books.

Phillips, Carol Brunson, and Louise Derman-Sparks. 1997. *Teaching/ Learning Anti-Racism: A Developmental Approach.* New York: Teachers College Press.

Point Made Learning. 2014. *I'm Not Racist . . . Am I?* Filmed in New York City, 1 hr. 33 min. Directed by Catherine Wigginton Greene. The Calhoun School Deconstructing Race Project. New York: Point Made Films. https://pointmadelearning.com /programs-and-services/film-screenings/im-not-racist-am-i.

Polacco, Patricia. 1998. *Thank You, Mr. Falker.* New York: Philomel Books.

Radical Math. www.radicalmath.org/main.php?id=SocialJusticeMath.

Radical Math. 2007. *Social Justice Math.* http://www.radicalmath.org /main.php?id=SocialJusticeMath.

Rethinking Schools. https://rethinkingschools.org.

Roediger, David R. 2005. *Working Toward Whiteness: How America's Immigrants Became White: The Strange Journey from Ellis Island to the Suburbs.* New York: Basic Books.

Rosenberg, Marshall B. 2003. *Nonviolent Communication: A Language of Life.* 2nd ed. Encinitas, CA: Puddledancer Press.

Ross, Loretta. J. 2019. "Speaking Up Without Tearing Down." *Learning for Justice* 61 (Spring): 19–22.

Sims Bishop, Rudine. 1990. "Mirrors, Windows, and Sliding Glass Doors." *Perspectives* 6 (3): ix. https://scenicregional.org/wp

-content/uploads/2017/08/Mirrors-Windows-and-Sliding-Glass
-Doors.pdf.

Singer, Isaac Bashevis. (1967) 1995. *Mazel and Schlimazel*. Illustrated by Margot Zemach. New York: Farrar, Straus & Giroux.

Singleton, Glenn E. 2015. *Courageous Conversations About Race*. Thousand Oaks, CA: Corwin.

Smithsonian Asian Pacific American Center. https://smithsonianapa.org.

Smithsonian National Museum of African American History and Culture. https://nmaahc.si.edu.

Smithsonian National Museum of the American Indian. https://americanindian.si.edu/visit/washington/nnavm.

So-Un, Kim. 2020. *Korean Children's Favorite Stories: Fables, Myths, and Fairy Tales*. Illustrated by Jeong Kyong-Sim. Rutland, VT: Tuttle.

Tansey, Molly, and Melissa Katz. 2015. "Teaching While White." *Learning for Justice*, April 30. www.learningforjustice.org/magazine/teaching-while-white.

Tatum, Beverly Daniel. 2017. *Why Are All the Black Kids Sitting Together in the Cafeteria?* New York: Basic Books.

Teaching for Change. www.teachingforchange.org.

The Trevor Project. www.thetrevorproject.org.

US Holocaust Memorial Museum. www.ushmm.org.

Voss, Christopher, with Tahl Raz. 2016. *Never Split the Difference: Negotiating as If Your Life Depended on It*. New York: HarperCollins.

UCLA Mathematics Project. https://centerx.gseis.ucla.edu/math-project.

Vygotsky, L. S. 1978. *Mind in Society: The Development of Higher Psychological Processes*. Cambridge, MA: Harvard University Press.

Wallace, David Foster. (2005) 2009. *This Is Water: Some Thoughts, Delivered on a Significant Occasion, About Living a Compassionate Life*. Boston: Little, Brown and Company.

Wilgoren, Jodi. 2001. "Algebra Project: Bob Moses Empowers Students." *New York Times*, Jan. 7, A4. Retrieved January 23, 2021, from https://www.nytimes.com/2001/01/07/education/algebra-project-bob-moses-empowers-students.html.

Wing Luke Museum of the Asian Pacific American Experience. www.wingluke.org.

Young, Ed. 1989. *Lon Po Po*. New York: Philomel.

## Works Cited

Zinn, Howard. 2009. *A Young People's History of the United States.*
    Adapted by Rebecca Stefoff. New York: Seven Stories Press.
Zinn Education Project. www.zinnedproject.org.

*Continuation of credits from the copyright page*:

Figures 2–1, 2–3, 5–2, 8–2: Excerpts from Common Core State Standards © Copyright 2010. National Governors Association Center for Best Practices and Council of Chief State School Officers. All rights reserved.

On p. 58, excerpt from *BC First Nations Land, Title, and Governance Teacher Resource Guide* (2019). http://www.fnesc.ca/wp/wp-content/uploads/2019/09/PUBLICATION-Governance-BCFNLTG-2019-09-17.pdf.

Figure 5–2: Reprinted with permission of Learning for Justice, a project of the Southern Poverty Law Center. https://www.learningforjustice.org/.